James Payn

Brick Church Memorial

James Payn

Brick Church Memorial

ISBN/EAN: 9783337004361

Printed in Europe, USA, Canada, Australia, Japan

Cover: Foto ©Lupo / pixelio.de

More available books at **www.hansebooks.com**

EXTERIOR OF THE OLD BRICK CHURCH IN BEEKMAN STREET

INTERIOR OF THE OLD CHURCH.

BRICK CHURCH MEMORIAL

CONTAINING

THE DISCOURSES DELIVERED BY DR. SPRING ON THE
CLOSING OF THE OLD CHURCH IN BEEKMAN
ST., AND THE OPENING OF THE NEW
CHURCH ON MURRAY HILL;

THE DISCOURSE DELIVERED

ON THE

Fiftieth Anniversary

OF HIS INSTALLATION AS PASTOR OF THE BRICK CHURCH;

WITH

THE PROCEEDINGS OF THE

MEMORIAL MEETING,

AND

THE DISCOURSE PREACHED ON THE OCCASION

OF

MRS. SPRING'S DECEASE.

NEW YORK:
M. W. DODD, PUBLISHER,
No. 506 BROADWAY.
1861.

Entered according to Act of Congress, in the year 1861,

By M. W. DODD,

In the Clerk's Office of the District Court of the United States, for the Southern District of New York.

NEW YORK:
PRINTED BY EDWARD O. JENKINS,
20 NORTH WILLIAM ST.

CONTENTS.

	PAGE.
DEPARTURE FROM THE BEEKMAN STREET CHURCH.	7
DEDICATION OF THE NEW CHURCH	45
FIFTIETH ANNIVERSARY DISCOURSE	81
PROCEEDINGS AT THE MEMORIAL MEETING	129
DISCOURSE ON THE DEATH OF MRS. SPRING	215

MEMORIAL OF GOD'S GOODNESS.

A DISCOURSE;

DELIVERED ON THE 25th OF MAY, 1856, AS THE CLOSING SERMON IN THE OLD BRICK CHURCH IN BEEKMAN STREET.

MEMORIAL OF GOD'S GOODNESS.

"We have thought of thy loving-kindness, O God, in the midst of thy temple. That ye may tell it to the generation following; for this God is our God, for ever and ever; he will be our guide even unto death."—PSALM xlviii. 9-14.

THE present service closes the public worship of God in an edifice where it has been enjoyed for 88 years. For whatever purposes this hallowed ground may be hereafter employed, experience has convinced us that it is no longer a fit place for religious worship. We have admitted this conviction reluctantly; we have resisted it too long. It is now forced upon us by considerations which we have no doubt God approves, and the best interests of his kingdom demand.

With the future we have less to do, on the present occasion, than with the past. The Brick Presbyterian Church has, from its origin, occupied a position sufficiently prominent to justify, even in the eyes of the men of the world, some historical notices, which may, perhaps, be viewed with interest by others as well as ourselves.

It requires no great labor and very little research to furnish the historical outlines of a Christian congregation, which dates back only 88 years. The first account we have of Presbyterianism in this city, is the combination of several Presbyterian families from England, Scotland, Ireland, France, and New England, in the year 1706, who were in the habit of assembling together on the Lord's day, in a private house, and conducting their religious services without the aid of any Christian minister. The following year they worshipped occasionally in the Dutch church in Garden street, and, in the year 1716, formed themselves into a regular Presbyterian church, under the stated ministry of the Rev. James Anderson, a native of Scotland. For three years this infant church assembled for public worship in the City Hall, then on the corner of Nassau and Wall streets; and in 1719, they erected the first Presbyterian church in Wall street, out of which was formed the Church of the Seceders in Cedar street, under the pastoral charge of the Rev. Dr. Mason the elder, and also the Brick church in Beekman street. The corner stone of this edifice was laid in the autumn of the year 1766, and on the first of January, 1768, it was opened for public worship, by a discourse from the Rev. Dr. Rodgers, its first pastor. The congregations worshipping in Wall street and in

Beekman street remained for a series of years *one church*, under the same associated pastorate, **the same** Board of Trustees, and the same bench **of** Ruling Elders. This identity of interest was preserved during the whole of the Revolutionary war, and down to the year 1809. During the war, these two Presbyterian churches were the objects of the special vengeance and indignity of the enemy. The church in Wall street was converted into barracks, and the Brick church into a hospital—defaced, stripped of their interior, and left in ruins, and the parsonage house burned **to** the ground. **On the return of peace, and** while these edifices were being **repaired,** the con**gregations statedly worshipped in St.** George's **and St. Paul's,** through the unsolicited and generous courtesy of the vestry of Trinity church. After having been repaired at great expense, the Brick church was reopened in June, 1784, by a discourse from Dr. Rodgers, from the words **of** the Psalmist, "I was glad when they said unto me, Let us go into the house of the Lord." The ministers successively associated with Dr. Rodgers, **after** the conclusion **of** the war, were the Rev. James Wilson, **from** Scotland, the **Rev.** John McKnight, and the Rev. Samuel Miller. These congregations, in their united capacity, and for many years after the present pastor of **the** Brick church came to the city, established and sustained a large parochial school, in Nassau, between Liberty and Cedar streets, and relinquished their funds for this object to the Public School directors, on the expressed condition that no child whom they should recommend should be excluded, and that the Bible should be daily read in the schools.

Serious inconveniences were found to attend the arrangement of this collegiate charge; and by an amicable stipulation, in the year 1809, the congregations, till then united, were formed into separate and distinct churches;—the Rev. Dr. Rodgers retaining his relation to both, and the Rev. Dr. Miller the stated pastor of the church in Wall street—Dr. McKnight voluntarily resigning his connexion with both churches.

Such was the state of the Brick church the year before the ordination and installation of the present pastor. The eldership consisted of men well known, both in civil and ecclesiastical life, and venerable for age and character. They were Abraham Vangelder, John Thompson, William Ogilvie, Benjamin Egbert, Thomas Frazer, John Bingham, John Mills, and Samuel Osgood, to which were added, shortly after the separation of the churches, William Whitlock, Richard Cunningham, Rensselaer Havens, and John Adams. While all these gentlemen were men of worth and influence, the ruling spirit among them, and the man eminent for discernment, practical wisdom, ardent piety, and vigorous action, was *John Mills*.

The age and infirmities of Dr. Rodgers had released him from all duty, and the great object of the church now was to secure the services of a stated pastor. There were divisions among them arising from the separation previously referred to, from ancient feuds, personal animosity, and political excitement. A call was presented to the Rev. Dr. John McDowell, of Elizabethtown, in New Jersey, which, though sustained by a large majority of the congregation, he declined accepting. Subsequently a call was presented to the Rev. Dr. Andrew Yates, of East Hartford, Connecticut, and though unanimous, was declined; Dr. Yates giving the preference to the Professorship of Moral Philosophy in Union College. Three efforts were subsequently made to induce the congregation to call the Rev. Lyman Beecher, then of East Hampton, Long Island; but for want of harmony, this measure was abandoned. Subsequently, in May, 1810, the Session deputed two of their number to procure the services of the Rev. Dr. Speece, of Virginia, on trial; this effort was also unsuccessful. At the same meeting they also appointed the same committee " to proceed to Philadelphia, during the sessions of the General Assembly, and make application to any of the Presbyterian ministers that may be convened there, whose piety and talents would, in their judgment, render him acceptable to the congregation, and earnestly solicit such minister to make the church a visit of two or three Sabbaths, with a view to a permanent settlement as pastor; and in case they should not find any minister there suitably qualified, that they make inquiry of the ministers present; and if they receive well-grounded information respecting any minister whose piety and talents would probably make him acceptable to the congregation, that they take such measures for procuring a visit from such minister as they may think proper." There is no record on the minutes of the Session of the action of this committee, and no report of the results of their appointment.

At a meeting of the Session, on the 28th of May, 1810, the first resolution was adopted which relates to your present pastor. He had not a single acquaintance in the congregation, nor does he know by whom, nor by what means his name was presented to the Session. He had passed through the city the preceding week, and preached a single discourse in the church in Cedar street, under the care of the late Dr. John B. Romeyn, and who was then in Philadelphia. While there, a spectator of the transactions of the Assembly, the Session passed the resolution inviting him to supply the pulpit. He accepted this invitation, and occupied the pulpit the first Sabbath in June, preaching in the morning from the words, "Wherefore come ye out from among them, and be ye separate, and touch not the unclean thing, and I will be a father unto you, and ye shall be my sons and daughters, saith the Lord Almighty;" and in the evening, to a crowded audience, from the words, "By the grace of God, I am what I am." I hold in my hand the identical discourses which I then preached, and have often been filled with wonder that these **two jejune and puerile discourses should have decided the question on** which so **many interests depended for time and** eternity. **But the hand of God was in the** whole procedure. At *the close of the morning service, and in the church*, the Session **had** a meeting, at which Dr. Rodgers presided, and which the deacons and trustees were invited to attend, at which they unanimously resolved that notice be given from **the** pulpit, at **the** close of the afternoon and evening service, **that the** congregation assemble **the** next **day to** take **into** consideration the **propriety of** making out **a call** for Mr. Gardiner **Spring to** become the stated **pastor of the Brick church.**

On the following **day** that meeting was held, the **Rev.** Dr. Milledoler, then **the** pastor of the church in Rutgers street, presiding, and a unanimous call was made out for the proposed candidate. I was greatly embarrassed by this unexpected invitation. A call had already been presented to me from the church in Andover, Massachusetts, from the Park Street church in Boston, and at the same time I had been requested to receive a call from the church in New Haven. The elders of the Brick church were urgent for a prompt and immediate decision, on account of the peculiar state of the congregation; and though I did not formally answer the call till the 6th of July, I gave to Mr. John Mills, the leading ruling elder, such intimations of my purpose that they had a right to consider me, and did consider me, as their minister. It appeared to my own mind the call of the Great Head of the church to a field of labor too important to be compared with others, and too unequivocal to be misunderstood. Unfitted for it as I was, yet encouraged to believe that I should have strength according to my day, I accepted the solemn charge, and was ordained by the Presbytery of New York, and installed the pastor of this people on the 8th of August, 1810. Of the Presbytery by which I was ordained,* consisting of Rev.

---

* Among those who were subsequently received into it, the following ministers also sleep in the dust:—Rev. William Boardman, Rev.

Dr. Rodgers, Rev. George Faitoute, Rev. Peter Fish, Rev. Philip Milledoler, Rev. Samuel Miller, Rev. John B. Romeyn, and the Rev. Ezra Stiles **Ely,** not one remains.

The fathers, where are they? and the younger prophets do not live forever. The distinguished individuals to whom I was under the greatest obligations, so long as they remained members of the Presbytery, were the Rev. Dr. Miller and the Rev. Dr. Perrine, both of whom filled the **office** of Professor of Church History and Government in our theological seminaries, and died **full** of years and full of honors. Their **uniform** friendship, their kind and gentleman-like deport**ment toward me,** their wise counsels, their active assistance **in** my arduous work, the interest they took in my usefulness, and the influence they exerted in my favor in seasons of solicitude, conflict

John Teasman, Rev. Henry Blatchford, Rev. Philip M. Whelpley, Rev. Samuel Whelpley, Rev. John B. Romeyn, Rev. Mathias Bruen, Rev. Henry P. Strong, Rev. Mathew L. R. Perrine, Rev. Joseph S. Christman, Rev. Henry Hunter, Rev. Elias Crane, Rev. Daniel Newell, Rev. Seymour P. Funk, Rev. Stephen N. Rowan, Rev. E. W. Baldwin, Rev. Daniel Carroll, Rev. Joseph Sanford, Rev. Henry White, Rev. George W. Perkins, Rev. Erskine Mason, Rev. Truman Norton, Rev. A. J. Graham, Rev. John Little, Rev. S. Larned, Rev. E. Holt, Rev. Walter King, Rev. Ward Stafford, Rev. Flavel S. Mines, Rev. **Isaac Lewis, Rev. F.** Chamberlain, Rev. **Albert Judson, Rev. George Bourne, Rev.** Robert Birch, Rev. Moses C. Searl, Rev. **Charles M. Oakly, Rev. George** Carrington, Rev. John Anderson, Rev. Nathaniel S. Prime, **Rev. Ichabod S. Spencer,** and Rev. Samuel E. Cornish.

and depression, demand from me this public and grateful acknowledgment.

During the first year of my ministry, I was constrained by necessity to the preparation of those discourses which I could most easily prepare. My subjects were such as were most familiar to my own mind, rather than those which were demanded by the character and condition of the congregation. But no sooner did it please God to give me the confidence of the people, than topics were carefully selected with a more special regard to the indications of divine providence, and the wants of those to whom I was called to minister. Both the elders and the people expected from me discourses that were addressed to the *popular ear and taste.* There was a standard of preaching and a feeling on this subject which tried and embarrassed me, and which led to a carefully prepared discourse from the words, "Speak unto us smooth things." God was pleased to put honor upon this discourse, and to produce the conviction on the minds of those who heard it, that the preacher's business is to *preach His truth*, and leave the consequences with Him, and that instead of aiming to *please men*, his great aim ought to be to *please God*, who trieth the hearts.

There was at that time prevalent in the city a sort of hybrid theology, half Arminian and half

Antinomian—tinctured with the views of "Marshal on Sanctification," on the one hand, and the ritualism of High Church Episcopacy on the other —which, young as I was, I felt myself called on to investigate and resist. In the main, it was evangelical and Calvinistic, but it was hyper-Calvinism, and not that *kind* of Calvinism which is taught in the Bible. Some of my own people were not a little imbued with it, and it led to a series of discourses on the "Discriminating traits of Christian character," in which the agitated questions were treated, not polemically, but practically. These discourses the Great Head **of the** church condescended to attend with his blessing, and to make the means of disturbing false hopes, **and** bringing many persons out of darkness into his marvellous light.

It was the preparation of these discourses which first directed my own thoughts to the discussion of subjects in *a series of discussions*, comprising from twenty to thirty discourses on the same general topic, so many of which have been delivered in this sanctuary, and subsequently found their way to the press. The most important of the series was that which, in the order of time, immediately followed **the** discussions on Christian characteristics. It comprised a system of theology, and consisted of more than one hundred discourses. It was the great effort **of my** life. The preparation of these discourses occupied more than three years of laborious and continuous study and preaching. Very many of them were delivered on the evening of the Lord's day, and to very large audiences. Nor do I know that any series of sermons preached by me have been listened to with greater interest, or have been more extensively useful. It was a system of theology not prepared for the schools, but for the people. And while it blinked no hard questions, save those which the word of God bids us to let alone, its main object was to show the bearing of every truth upon the conscience and heart; to exalt God, and to lay the sinner, humbled and without excuse, trembling, yet hoping, at the foot of the cross. The *practical application* of every doctrine was the most labored part of almost every discourse; nor have I ever preached to more solemn audiences, nor with more evident tokens of the divine favor and presence, than when preaching some of these discourses. One of these, I well recollect, cost six weeks' labor; and I mention this, not for the discouragement, but the encouragement of those ministers who, in the vigor of their days, are willing to be *working men.*

My preparations for the Sabbath have been habitually, almost always and uniformly made *in season;* never, to my recollection, except in two instances, deferred to the last day of the week; nor do I know of any better way of gaining time, labor, knowledge, and health, than such an arrangement. One little circumstance, in connection with the series of theological discourses, deserves here to be mentioned, that gave interest to them. During their delivery in the winter season, in addition to the Thursday evening lecture, there was established a Bible-class, or rather a theological class, in "the old Session-room," comprising all of both sexes who chose to attend, for the purpose of reviewing, examining, and enforcing, by question and answer, the discourse of the preceding Lord's day. It was a large class, often numbering more than a hundred, and though it consisted of gentlemen in professional and literary life, of merchants, and mechanics, and teachers, and ladies of greater and less distinction; and though all liberty was allowed of proposing questions on subjects of difficulty, it was a *religious* class, and was understood to be a *religious* service. There was no restraint, but the most unembarrassed and cheerful discussion; yet there was no rudeness, no frivolity. It was one of the most interesting and solemn services of the season, and gave solemnity and interest to all our other services. God was with us by the influence of his sacred Spirit. And when we came to the practical application of any such great doctrine as man's depravity, the sovereignty of God, the nature of holiness, the nature and necessity of regeneration, the great atonement of his Son, and the retribution of his punitive justice, many a time did proud heads droop, and the question was answered by a tear. Men and women are now living, who, though widely scattered, will never forget this beautiful service. And here commenced the first memorable outpouring of God's Spirit upon this people. Not far from *thirty* of this class, principally young, where turned from the power of Satan unto God, some of whom have died in faith and hope, some of whom live to exert a Christian influence, and some of whom are eminent for their usefulness in the gospel ministry.

God had graciously given testimony to the word of his grace, as here preached, at earlier periods. The thought has no doubt often crossed the minds of reflecting Christians that those who have occupied a place on the earth during the last fifty years, have lived in a remarkable age of the world, not only as it respects science and the arts, and the progress of civil society, but in regard to the cause of vital piety. The period, commencing with the year 1792, and terminating with 1842, was a memorable period in the history of the American Church. Scarcely any portion of it, except the high church Episcopalian and the Unitarian churches of Massachusetts, but were graciously visited by copious effusions of the Holy Spirit. From north to south, and from east to west, our male, and more especially our female academies, our colleges, and our churches, drank largely of this fountain of living waters. It was my privilege to enter upon the course of academical life not far from the meridian of this bright day. There were no subjects that interested my mind more deeply when I began my ministry among this people, than those revivals of religion which passed over the land of my boyhood. This interest increased with time, and official labors and responsibility, and exercised a most important influence upon my whole course. **Sparse clouds of mercy had** been hovering over the congregation during the first four years of my ministry, and not a few, especially of those in middle life, had been brought into the kingdom of God. The year 1814 was a year of severe labor and deep solicitude; as it drew towards its close, of great discouragement and depression. It seemed to me that I must abandon my post, and that neither my mind, my heart, nor my health was adequate to its constantly accumulating duties. My intellectual resources seemed to be exhausted, and drained dry. Many a time, after preaching, did I remain long in the pulpit that I might not encounter the faces of the people as I left the church; and many a time, when I left it, did I feel that

I could never preach another sermon. Yet I labored on week after week, without discovering to what extent the Spirit of God was carrying forward his own noiseless work. I perceived nothing to encourage me but an unusual enlargement and urgency in prayer, a great facility in the selection of fitting themes for the pulpit, and more freedom and earnestness in declaring the whole counsel of God. God remarkably interposed to relieve my mind from its depression, and gave me such enlarged and delightful views of his truth, that my whole ministry received a new and cheered impulse. It was easy, also, to perceive that the spirit of grace and supplication was being poured out upon the people. The weekly prayer-meeting and the weekly lecture were full of interest. Days of fasting and prayer were occasionally observed, and a Saturday evening prayer-meeting was established by the young men of the congregation. Our Sabbaths became deeply solemn and affecting; we watched for them like those who watch for the morning, and I verily believe we anticipated them with greater pleasure and expectation than the sons and daughters of earth ever anticipated their brightest jubilee. This was the first strongly marked revival of God's work among this people; and I take this notice of it because it was so emphatic an expression of God's goodness to your young minister. Poor a thing as I have been, and still continue to be, it was this work of grace which made me what I am; which gave me entirely new views of the great objects of the ministry, and made my work my joy. I loved it before, but never so ardently as then. But for this early season of mercy, during the summer of 1814, I do not see how I could ever have remained among you. It was the Lord's doing, and it is marvellous in our eyes. The ingathering was not great, but it was the finest of the wheat. I may not mention their names.

This was but the beginning of the days of mercy. The commencement of the year 1815 was the dawning of a still brighter day. The last Sabbath of the old year and the evening services of that Sabbath will be long remembered. Eight or ten persons, during the following week, were found to be awake, and in earnest for their salvation. The whole winter was a day of the right-hand of the Most High. The cloud of mercy extended itself through the following spring, and summer, and autumn. In the month of November the Bible-class was reorganized, the Saturday evening prayer-meeting was renewed, and God appeared to take the work into his own hands. There were complaint and hostility; there were not wanting apprehensions in the minds of some of the pastors and churches in the city that the work savored more of fanaticism than intelligent and sober thought. But the apprehensions were groundless. The blessing was near; the sacred influence was silent as the dew of heaven. There was no outbreak and no disorder. There was prayer. There was solemn and earnest preaching. There were unexpected and unthought-of instances of seriousness among the gay and frivolous, in the families of the rich as well as the poor, among the immoral as well as the moral, and many were the instances of conversion to God. The third Thursday of January was set apart by about thirty members of the church as a day of fasting, humiliation, and prayer. It was in a private house in the rear of St. Paul's, in Church street; and such a day I never saw before, and have never seen since. It was closed under strong and confident expectation that God was near, and that his Spirit **was** about largely to descend upon the people. **And** so it was. A delightful impulse was given **to the** work by this day of prayer. The promise was made good, "Before they call I will answer, and while they are yet speaking I will hear." The weekly lecture, attended on the evening of that day was perhaps the most solemn service of my ministry. The subject of the discourse was suggested by the words, "Marvel **not** that I said unto you, Ye must be born again." God was with the hearers and the preacher; his Spirit moved them as the trees of the forest are moved by a mighty wind. There is good reason to believe that the minds of more than one hundred persons **were** deeply impressed with a sense of their lost condition as sinners, and their need of an interest in Christ, on that evening. Enemies were silenced; members of other churches came among us to see and mark the character of the work for themselves, and all classes were constrained to confess, "This is the finger of God." Between one and two hundred attended the meetings for religious inquiry and conversation, and deep solemnity pervaded the whole people. There was great eagerness for religious instruction, and great **satisfaction in the soul**-humiliating and soul-encouraging **doctrines of the** cross. The **work was** rapid. **The period of** awakening **and** conviction in many instances was very short—so short that older Christians began to doubt the genuineness of such conversions. There was no reason for the doubt. Some of the brightest and most enduring Christians amongst us were those very persons whose conversion was almost as sudden as that of Saul of Tarsus. The gathering of this protracted harvest was rich, consisting **sometimes** of thirty and forty, and at one communion **of** more than seventy, filling **the broad** aisle **of the** church—a lovely spectacle to God, angels, **and** men.

There have been five seasons of the especial outpouring of God's Spirit upon this people during the ministry of their present pastor. They were interspersed between the years 1812 and 1834, more or less copious, but always seasons of delightful refreshing from the presence of the Lord. If the tree is known by its fruit, they are proved to have been the fruit of God's Spirit. The subjects of this work of grace have, in almost all instances, run well; they have turned out intelligent and active Christians. Many of them have been called to their last earthly rest; nor shall I forget the blessedness and the blessed scenes of their last hours. Many of them are ministers of the gospel, and more the wives of ministers. Many of them are teachers and superintendents of Sabbath-schools. Many of them are ruling elders and deacons in other churches, while some remain in the honorable fulfilment of these offices among ourselves. Very many of them are scattered through this wide land, and distant churches and the distant wilderness are made glad *for them.* I never was so gratefully impressed with this fact, and with the high privilege of preaching the gospel in this sanctuary, as on an unexpected tour through Western New York, and the Western States on the Upper Mississippi. Everywhere I met those who remembered the young minister and the Old Session-room. I heard of the death of some far away; and it was affecting to learn that in their last hours their thoughts of grateful praise were turned toward these scenes of mercy.

It will be found by an inspection of our records, that after the separation of the Brick and Wall Street churches, and before the installation of the present pastor, the Session were faithfully employed in acts of *painful discipline*. Church discipline is not less truly an ordinance of God than church communion. No church can prosper that connives at heresy or immorality among its communicants. This unwelcome duty was faithfully pursued for several years after my settlement among this people, and has been discharged with perfect unanimity ever since. In the early part of my ministry there were some avowed infidels in the church, who were the disciples of Paine and Palmer; there were, also, avowed Universalists; there have been, from time to time, immoral men and licentious, whom no means could reclaim, and they have been cast out. It has often been at great sacrifice of feeling, and some of interest and influence, that these acts of discipline have been performed; but, however reluctantly and cautiously, it is a work which has been done. There have also been evils in the church at large with which the Brick church has sympathized, and in the pressure of which it has endeavored to exert a healing and conservative influence. The great schism in the Presbyterian church in the United States, which **issued** in the **excision** of so many churches in Western New York, was one in which this church took no part, and which it endeavored to prevent. We saw and felt that there **were** errors in doctrine and in church polity **that** were at variance with our standards; **but it was our** judgment that there was a constitutional remedy for them, and that it ought **to have** been adopted. We had no confidence in the men who were the leaders of **the New School** party, and believed that their aims were to secure exclusive power; but we could not believe that the mass of their followers were not true to our standards, **and** could never be persuaded that such a wholesale excision, without **any** previous trial, **was** consistent with sound **Presb**yterianism. Yet all our **sympathies in doctrine and in polity** were with the Old School. We **were crowded** to the wall, and called on to decide whether or not **our allotment** should be cast with the New School, who had abandoned themselves to leaders with whom we had no sort of sympathy, or with the Old School, with whom our doctrinal views and views of church order were in unison, while we disapproved of their excinding acts. Nor did we long hesitate, but formed our decision, after having frankly expressed our dissent from their measures, to remain with the excinding party. This was an unhappy division, though overruled for good. There are hundreds of as good men and sound Presbyterians in the excinded churches as are to be found among ourselves; and when time, that great healer, shall have purged them of the unhallowed leaven, and fostered a more fraternal spirit in both these branches of the great Presbyterian family in this land, we doubt not they will once more become united and harmonious. Blame was imputed to us by both parties for **our** neutral course; but we did not think it neutral. Our decision to remain with the Old School **was prompt and firm, and** not less prompt and firm was our *Protest* against its excinding **acts, and that Protest now stands on the records of the Presbytery.** We **did** not deem this a neutral course; nor could we, with an honest conscience, **have** adopted any other, without fomenting still further disunion, and forming, as was seriously thought of, a third party in a church which ought ever to have been *one*.

In those great and benevolent enterprises for which the age in which we live has been distinguished, it has been the privilege of the Brick church to bear her part. Taking the forty-six years **of** my pastorate together, no church in **the land** has given more bountifully to the cause of **domestic** and foreign missions. **It has done** not a little also in the work of educating poor and pious young men for the gospel ministry. Boston, New York, Elizabethtown, Princeton, and the West and far West to this day have eminent ministers, in the Congregational, Presbyterian, and Dutch Reformed churches, who were beneficiaries of this church.

Of God's goodness toward myself, I might write volumes without exhausting the theme. My own life and the life of her he so early gave me, have been spared to us, while the great mass of the companions of our youth among this people sleep among the dead. It is a coincidence which an old man may be pardoned for taking notice of, that *this day* on which we now meet, completes the *fiftieth year* of our married life. It was on the *twenty-fifth* of May, 1806, the Lord's day, that we were united in bonds not to be severed but by death. This *twenty-fifth* of May, 1856, also the Lord's day, celebrates our "golden wedding," and we are both well pleased in thus inviting you to this religious celebration, which looks back upon so many interesting facts in the narrative of our pilgrimage. Thirteen of our children were born in the midst of you, and baptized in this house of God; and you have generously borne with their failings and ours. Six of the fifteen have died since our connection with you, and you have sympathized with our trials, and liberally provided for our wants and theirs. Your unexpected bounty to us two years ago, when I was thousands of miles from you, and knew not of the generous arrangement so nobly made in order to relieve the solicitude of the evening of our days, demands this grateful and public acknowledgment.*

---

* The bounty here referred to, and so unexpectedly dispensed, will the better appear from the following documents:

NEW YORK, *7th June*, 1854.

PURSUANT to public notice given from the pulpit, a meeting of the male members and stated hearers of the Brick Presbyterian church in Beekman street, was held this day in the church, to consider and determine, agreeably to said notice, upon a subject of interest to the congregation, embraced in the eighth section of the act to provide for the Incorporation of Religious Societies, in relation to Minister's salaries.

On motion, SAMUEL MARSH, Esq., was called to **preside as Chairman, and Moses Allen, Esq., was appointed** Secretary.

The notice under which the meeting was called having been read, the following resolutions were offered, and, after having been duly considered, were unanimously adopted:

I. **In consideration of the arduous labors** of our excellent **pastor for a long series of years, at a salary below the a**verage amount paid to many **clergymen** of this city, to remunerate, **in some** measure, his past services, and more adequately compensate them in future, *Resolved*,That the salary of the Rev. Dr. Spring hereafter be fixed at five thousand dollars per annum, commencing with the present fiscal year.

II. *Resolved*, That the preceding resolution be communicated to the Board of Trustees, and that they be requested to ratify the same, agreeably to said act.

III. *Resolved*, That Horace Holden, Samuel Marsh, Moses Allen, Guy Richards, and Ira Bliss, be a committee to communicate these resolutions to the Rev. Dr. Spring, and to express to him the undiminished confidence and affection of this church and congregation, and their earnest prayer that God may long preserve him to be His minister to this people.

SAMUEL MARSH, *Chairman.*

Moses ALLEN, *Secretary.*

At a meeting of the Board of Trustees of the Brick Presbyterian church, on the 13th of June, 1854, Mr. Holden presented to the Board a certified **copy of** the proceedings of a meeting of the congregation, held in the church, on Wednesday, **the** 7th day **of** June n't, which was read, and ordered to be entered on the minutes.

Whereupon, on motion, it was unanimously *Resolved*,That this Board **do approve of,** and hereby ratify and confirm, the aforesaid proceedings of the **congregation, fixing the** salary **of the** Rev. Dr. Spring at five thousand dollars per annum, **to commence the** first day of May last.

A true copy from the Minutes.

THOMAS EGGLESTON, *Clerk.*

My labors among you have been, for the year past, curtailed **and embarrassed** by the visitation of God. The **world** of sense **has** been for the most **part** shut out from my **obstructed vision;**

NEW YORK, 13*th June*, 1854.

REV. DR. SPRING :—

DEAR SIR : The undersigned have been appointed **a committee to** communicate to **you the** accompanying resolutions, passed unanimously at a meeting of **the congregation,** and subsequently in like manner ratified and confirmed by the Board of Trustees.

It affords **us** great pleasure to discharge this duty, and it **is** only embittered with the regret that this act of justice **has** been **so** long delayed, much of which delay may be chargeable to our own negligence or forgetfulness, not to use **a** harsher name.

It is gratifying to be able to state, that on this occasion but one sentiment pervaded the entire meeting; not the slightest dissent was manifested in thought, word, or deed. It was the spontaneous expression of grateful feelings from full and thankful hearts.

For almost half a century you have occupied the same post, and the same sphere of labor and of duty.

Some of us have sat under your ministry for more than forty years, and during that long period can bear testimony to your untiring industry, your unbending integrity in the exhibition of gospel truth amid conflicts and parties, and your entire devotion to the appropriate duties of the ministry

We feel, too, that it is neither flattery to you, nor vain-boasting in us, but a thankful expression of gratitude to God, to say, that yours has not been an unprofitable ministry, nor your influence been confined to this church. We can see traces of your faithful preaching, marked by the divine Spirit, not only in our city and vicinity, but in almost every state of this vast republic; and we expect, if we are ever so happy as to **arrive** at our Father's house on high, to meet multitudes there of those whom neither **you nor we** have known in the flesh, brought home to glory through your instrumentality.

It is a source of delightful reflection to us, that in the early evening of your **days, after so long a ministry among us, you** retain the undiminished confidence and affection **of your whole people, an** affection as warm and fresh as crowned the day when first you devoted your youthful prime in this church, to Christ and his cause.

Our beloved pastor! these expressions but feebly represent our own sincere emotions.

We would humbly commend you to the Great Head of the church, and earnestly pray that He may preserve you yet for many years to come, to preach the everlasting gospel to this people—that He may make you perfect, stablish, strengthen, settle you ; and finally, when our warfare is accomplished, that He may receive you and us to that blessed **communion where our love** shall be for ever perfect, and our joy for ever full.

Respectfully and affectionately,

HORACE HOLDEN,
SAMUEL MARSH,
MOSES ALLEN,   } *Committee.*
IRA BLISS,
GUY RICHARDS,

a heavy cloud has hung upon it, which I know not will ever be so removed that I can labor among you with comfort or usefulness. I bow to this visitation; I am not unhappy under it. I have no doubt of the care and faithfulness of our heavenly Father in thus laying his rod upon me. I have never been unhappy in my work, but have greatly rejoiced in it as in every view my chosen service; thankful above all earthly things that God was pleased to put me into the ministry. I have never regretted the choice for a moment. I have found trials in it, but not one more than was required by the imperfections of my own character, my position, and my usefulness; and were I now in the bloom of youth and secular promise, of all employments in the world I would choose that of a minister of the gospel. With all my unworthiness, I would go to the throne and say, "Here, Lord, am I; send *me!*" This conviction grows upon me as my infirmity gradually disqualifies me for the labors to which I have been accustomed. I cannot speak of the glad emotions which fill my heart, as, in the suspension of my more vigorous studies, I sometimes look over the thousands of manuscripts I have been allowed to prepare, and reflect upon the *privilege* of having been permitted to utter so much precious truth to this beloved people. It is a delightful view to my own mind, that, with all my deficiencies, God has not permitted me to be a *loiterer* in his vineyard, and that, however imperfectly, my work has not been negligently done. What my motives have been another day will show. Of one thing I am confident, that I have been devoted to it, regardless of all other vocations. My great cause of solicitude now is that I shall wane, and fade, and faint, and die "of having nothing to do." I find these days of unreading and unstudious repose the greatest trial of my life, except my sins. I ask your indulgence, your sympathy, and your prayers, that God would give me a cheerful mind, and so direct me in the employment of my time that my life may not become a burden, and that I may not be a cumberer of the ground. Yet, I may not, I do not, distrust him. Because thou hast been my help; therefore, under the shadow of thy wings will I rejoice.

And now, in this brief review, what shall we say? One thought forces itself upon your minds and my own. It relates to a theme on which I have so often dwelt in this sacred desk: The *goodness of God*, how wonderful it is! The rising and setting sun proclaim it, and every star of the dark night. Like the milky way, it fills the heavens with its whiteness; and like the rainbow painted on the clouds, it spans them with its prismatic beauty. The atmosphere we breathe is surcharged with it, and it **is** conducted off in its ten thousand electric forms. Every bird, fish, and worm, every buzzing insect, every plant and flower, and every blade of grass inhale it. Every sea, every lake and fountain, every river and stream and sparkling dew-drop, receive alike their riches and their beauty from this uncreated source. How much more richly and purely, then, does it flow here in the sanctuary where all its streams **are** confluent, and from the mountain-tops of Zion send gladness through the city of our God! We cannot comprehend **the love that brought the** Lord of Glory to **the manger and the** cross; that **here** proclaims **the glad tidings of great joy,** and that **sends** forth his Spirit **to call** the wanderers home. **" O that** men would praise the Lord for his goodness!" "How great is thy goodness to them that fear thee, to them that put their trust in thee before the sons of men!"

I love this place where I now stand—

"Here my best friends, my kindred, dwell;
Here **God,** my Saviour, reigns."

Had **any one told** me twenty years ago that I should live to see it abandoned **as a** place of religious worship, I should have thought **him** a romancer, **if** not a madman; yet **the** hour of abandonment has come. On an occasion like the present, something is due to this ancient sanctuary. The speaker stands here for the last time; and you, beloved friends, meet for the last time in the consecrated place where we have so often assembled for the worship of God. As before intimated, I am not ignorant of the defects of my ministry. Yet have I this thankful conviction, that, so far as I have known it, I have not shunned to declare the whole council of God. If I have not, testify against me this day. We call upon you to witness, we call upon the sainted spirits of the departed to witness, we make our appeal to the walls of this hallowed edifice, if the truth of God, detached from the systems of human philosophy, from the misnamed improvements and ultraisms of the age, and from the popular daubing with untempered mortar, has not been proclaimed from this pulpit. This house has also been greatly endeared to us as "the house of prayer," as "the house of prayer for all people." Many are the seasons which the living and the dead have here enjoyed, in sweet communion with God and one another. This house has been our thankful resort in prosperity; in adversity it has been our refuge. Here the aged and the young have come for the first and last time to commemorate the love of Christ at his table. Here our children have been baptized, and their children after them, and here we have wept and prayed together as God has called them from these earthly scenes. Here other generations have listened, as you now listen, and around this spot and beneath it are the sepulchres of the departed. I seem to stand to-day amid generations that are past, so vividly does my imagination people these seats with faces and forms whose place now knows them no more. Pleasant, yet mournful, are these reminiscences; memory has no associations more delightful than those which run by the waters of the sanctuary. This house has also been the stranger's home. Of this and of that man it shall be one day said, that "he was born here." Many a wanderer from other lands, and more from distant regions of our own broad territory, have here sought and made their peace with God; while many a backslider has been restored, amid scenes which have given joy to the angels of God, and told of the years of the right-hand of the Most High. Recollections of individual character and deep and tender interest gush upon us to-day, which, while we must suppress, are full of thankfulness and praise. "We have thought of thy loving-kindness, O God, in the midst of thy temple," that "we may tell it to the generations following," and that "this God is our God, for ever and ever, and will be our guide even unto death."

But our work and our privileges in this house of God here have an end. It is His voice which to-day says to us, "Arise ye, and depart hence, for this is not your **rest.**" We have occupied it too long; and although it has been **for t**he benefit and enlargement of other congregations, it has been not **only to** the diminution of our strength, but to the injury of our habits as a people, and almost to the breaking up of our second service on the Sabbath. Notwithstanding the doubts of some, and the officious and uncalled-for interference of others, **we ourselves are** satisfied that this once tranquil and central **spot is no longer a** place of repose either for the preacher **or** the hearers. We have no longer the unobstructed privileges of the gospel. Our weekly lecture and our weekly prayer-meeting, as well as our Sabbath-school, are of necessity discontinued; while it is at no small inconvenience that a single religious service is sustained on the **Lord's day.** The question **has** been asked, Why not leave this church as a church for strangers, and **for the hotels and boarding-houses in** this part of **the city?** To this we have this conclusive answer, **We ourselves have proposed to do so.** At a meeting of the **Presbytery of New York, I** myself made **the** proposition to the churches that this congregation would subscribe $50,000 for that purpose, on condition that the other congregations would unite in raising the balance of $150,000. The Presbytery received the proposal **with** favor, and appointed a committee to take it into consideration. That committee reported against the proposed arrangement, and the Presbytery and the congregations dropped the subject.

We have come to the conclusion, therefore, **to quit this edifice,** not indeed without difficulty, but deliberately. And **we owe** many thanks to those who, amid all the turmoil from without, all the foreign influence, and all the gradual dereliction from our services of our own congregation, have *stood by us* in this crisis of our history. For years we have been almost *in transitu ;* and it has put in requisition no small degree of attachment to the house of their fathers, and no small degree of Christian principle, to **make the sacrifices that have** been indispensable **to our continuance as a** well-organized department **in the house of God. While** none **of** us are without lingering attachments to these **ancient** courts, few if any among ourselves now question the expediency, the duty, of the removal. We have been a harmonious people for six and forty years; and we are now harmonious in this great and agitating question. And although we cannot say **that** we leave these walls without regret, we **can say** we leave them for conscience' sake, and **at the** bidding **of** our divine Leader. **The house does not** belong to *us*, but to *Him;* **and therefore we are bound to** husband the property entrusted to us, for the best interests of His kingdom. We bid it *adieu*, to follow the guidance of his providence, and pitch our tabernacle under the pillar and the cloud. These seats will no longer be occupied by us; this pulpit will henceforth be silent. To you who have long rejected the gospel as here proclaimed, it now makes its *last call.* Prayer will no longer ascend from this altar; the songs of this temple will now cease. Farewell, then, thou endeared house of God! thou companion and friend of my youth, thou comforter of my later years, thou scene of toil and of repose, of apprehension and of hope, of sorrow and of joy, of man's infirmity and of God's omnipotent grace, *farewell!* Sweet pulpit, farewell! Blessed altar, farewell! Throne of grace, as here erected, and where God no longer records his name, farewell!

But *not to Thee*, O thou that hearest prayer, thou God of Zion, who dost still dwell with man upon the earth—*not to Thee*, who hast said, "*Wherever* I record my name, I will come unto thee, and I will bless thee," do we say farewell! "The desire of our souls is to thy Name, and to the remembrance of Thee. Whom have we in heaven but *Thee*, and what is there on the earth that we desire beside thee?" Even now, at this late, this last hour, from the bottom of our hearts do we say, "If thy presence go not with us, carry us not up hence." If we forget Thee, ever blessed and adorable Saviour, or the church which thou hast purchased, **or** the Mount Zion where thou dwellest, let our right hand forget her cunning, let our tongue cleave to **the roof of** our mouth, if we prefer not Thee **and** these above our chief joy!

Nor, my beloved people, is it to *you* that your pastor says farewell. These brick walls and this plastered ceiling, and these pillars and seats, do not constitute the Brick Presbyterian church. Ye are these constituents, and "ye are our glory and joy." The winter of life is too near for me to have much personal interest in your arrangements for the future. My personal interests **and repose** would be the better consulted by remaining where **we are.** My **heart's desire and prayer to God, and my most vivid** hopes, **are for your usefulness** and benefit, rather than my **own.** I would **not** see you a dispersed people. And while it is with *concern* that I say this, it is with hope rather than fear. I would fain *live* to see you lengthening your cords and strengthening your stakes. But whether I **live or die, God** will assuredly **be** with you, and bring you **to the place of** his sanctuary. "**If I** shall find favor in his eyes, he will show **me both it and** his habitation. But **if** he say thus, **I have** no delight in thee, behold here **I am, let him do as** seemeth good unto him!" **Thus far he has led us** on in mercy.

These days of solicitude and agitation will soon

be over. "The root of Jesse" yet stands as an "ensign to the people, and his rest shall be glorious." Only take diligent heed and *be very courageous* to do his will, to love the Lord your God, and to walk in his ways, and to keep his commandments, and to cleave unto him, and to serve him with all your heart and all your soul, and his presence and blessing shall be with you and yours for a great while to come! The Lord bless you and keep you; the Lord cause his face to shine upon you, and be gracious unto you; the Lord lift up his countenance upon you, and give you peace! His name be upon you and your children! Amen and amen! And let all the people say, Amen!

EXTERIOR OF THE NEW BRICK CHURCH ON MURRAY HILL.

INTERIOR OF THE NEW CHURCH.

THE SANCTUARY.

A SERMON;

PREACHED ON THE 31st OF OCTOBER, 1858, AT THE
DEDICATION OF THE NEW BRICK CHURCH
ON MURRAY HILL.

THE SANCTUARY.

"Ye shall reverence my sanctuary."—LEVITICUS xix. 30.

STRONG has been the desire of him who addresses you to see this auspicious day; more strong than his expectations. The removal of a church hallowed by so many affecting associations as those concentrated around the place of our fathers' sepulchres; a church that has borne no insignificant part in our national history, and where so many distinguished men and fathers of the American Revolution worshipped; a church, the foundation of which was laid with their own hands; a church memorable for the power of God in the conversion of men, and endeared to so many now scattered over this broad land,—was an enterprise which none of us anticipated without misgivings of heart, and none counted on accomplishing without difficulty. These difficulties met us on every side; but "having obtained help of God, we continue to the present day," the same organized community with which such multitudes have identified their sweetest hopes, where their graces flourished, whence their prayers ascended, and on which they now look down in the gladness of anticipation and with the fervor of praise. We have no ordinary cause for thanksgiving to God, and for mutual gratulation, that, after an exile of two and a half years, we at length assemble in these courts.

We meet on this day of our holy solemnities to dedicate this edifice to Him to whose name and praise, we trust, it will ever be devoted. We would honor *Him*, by putting honor upon the institutions of his own appointment; He himself would have us reverence his sanctuary.

The subject of this discourse, therefore, is that one great word—

The SANCTUARY, comprising, as it does, the divine presence, its moral power, its benevolent influence, its conservative principles, and its social character.

We reverence it,

I. In the first place, AS THE HOUSE OF GOD.

When we come to it, we shut the door on the world, and think of the great and glorious Being who occupies it. It was his early promise, "In all places where I record my name, I will come unto thee, and I will bless thee." His presence consecrated the field and the stone where Jacob slept. It consecrated the bush on Horeb, and the "tabernacle of witness" in the wilderness. It consecrated the temple at Jerusalem as " an habitation for the mighty God of Jacob," and made its history the history of earth and heaven. It was holy ground, because God was there. No uncircumcised could enter it, nor any unclean thing be offered on its altars. When the Hebrews were exiles in a strange land, their harps hung upon the willows because they had no symbols of the divine presence. When their temple was pillaged and burnt, and the wall of their city broken down, and its palaces destroyed with fire, and they became tributary to foreign kings, their glory was departed, because the Shekinah was gone, and the God of Israel was no longer among them. And when, **in after times,** their temple was desecrated by all the rites of paganism, and the statue **of Jupiter was set up on** the altar of burnt **offering, it was no longer a** sanctuary. And **now, when** the proud Moslem sits **upon** the throne of David, and the mosque of Omar stands on Mount Zion, how emphatically is the lesson inculcated on the world, that the God of Israel dwells no longer in Jerusalem, no longer in Mount Gerizim, but with every assembly of worshippers gathered in his name.

This is the high privilege of every Christian sanctuary. If the pagan world reverences its temples as the dwelling-place of its deities, how much more ought Christians to look upon their sanctuaries as sacred in the sanctity of their Oracle, and the presence of their God.

Solemn thought, that the King eternal, immortal, and invisible, before whom the loftiest and the holiest are lost in amazement, bows his heavens and comes down to these earthly courts! Yet is it a thought that cheers us, because, while he comes in the splendor of his rectitude, he comes in the gushing tenderness of his compassions; while he comes to stamp disappointment and mockery on every hope which **rests not** on him, he comes as the **refuge and hope of the** lowly; and comes, **not so much** in the glory that encircled Sinai and made the prophet tremble, as in the winning loveliness, the blended and attractive glory, which shines in the face of Jesus Christ.

Well may we turn aside to see this great sight, "*God with us*," within the walls of an earthly temple. In lowly reverence we fall before this present Deity; the celestial here bending to the terrestrial; the unseen and all-seeing One dwelling in the framework which is **of man's device**. "How *dreadful* is this place!" yet how *delightful!* "**Surely this is** none other than the house **of God, and** the gate **of heaven!**" Well may all hearts shout with joy at the condescension of this reconciled God. The sanctuary is the presence-chamber of the King of kings; his own royal banqueting-house, and the "mountain **of his holiness.**" If we look into the book of nature, or into the revelations of conscience, or into the writings of human philosophy and the speculations of science, we find nothing that answers the question, **What and where is God?** It is an absolute, abstract Deity the human mind always thinks of, until he is revealed in the person of his Son. The sanctuary draws aside the veil, behind which the great Jehovah "dwells in the thick darkness." There we find the God whom we are not afraid to think of, and to hold fellowship with, and who, to all the varied attributes of greatness, adds those varied manifestations of goodness which command our submission, our filial love, our trusting confidence. No earthly joy and honor, no patronage of the rich and learned, **no crowded assemblies,** no arm of flesh, **no tokens of public favor, can** be to us instead of his **presence and glory. What are** all the **formality and gorgeousness** of worship, if He who is **a Spirit be not here** worshipped in spirit **and in truth?** What is all human teaching, with its well digested thoughts and charms of utterance, if God's own lips speak not, and the soft whispers of his love breathe not? Say to us, thou God of Zion, "My presence shall go with thee, and I will give thee rest!" **We** would behold the beauty of **the Lord,** as we have seen it in the sanctuary. Our prosperity depends **upon** the bright visions **of** his glory. **O that he** would **walk amid** the golden candlesticks, **and** make this place of his feet glorious! **The** inward tokens of his presence are the best **pledge that we** shall enjoy the outward tokens **of his favor. Give** us these, and there will not be wanting those who will say, "We will go with you, for we have heard the Lord is with you."

II. We reverence the **sanctuary**, in the second place, FOR ITS MORAL POWER.

Men are apostate and sinful. Sin has impoverished them. They have wants which nothing but unearthly resources can supply, "having no hope and without God in the world." Iniquity is their ruin. So long as iniquity rankles in their bosoms, it proves the sharpened tooth of the undying worm; the fires of perdition cannot be quenched, so long as men remain the victims of wickedness.

It is no marvel, therefore, that the most comprehensive purpose of the divine mind terminates in securing and perpetuating the interests of holiness. His works, his providence, together with the rich and varied manifestations of his great and glorious nature, ever have had for their object the great interests of holiness in the world in which we dwell. The mightiest movement his wisdom and love ever dictated aims at here constructing a highway that shall be called "the way of holiness." Holiness is the ultimate good. There is nothing better that God seeks after, and nothing else he has made such sacrifices to secure.

In the accomplishment of this great work the sanctuary has a part to perform, which can be performed by no other instrumentality. Where no vision is, the people perish. Men rarely become moral, never religious, dissociated and severed from the house of God. If the sanctuary has an interest in the happiness of men, it is a happiness that is inseparable from a holy and virtuous character. What it most seeks to promote is a character that God loves, a character that is progressively like his own, a character cherished by all that is binding in the obligations of law, all that is rich in the plenitude of grace, all that is tender in the sympathies of our great High Priest, and all that is stimulating in those "exceeding great and precious promises" whereby his people are made partakers of the divine nature. Do you ask how the sanctuary effects this great object? we answer, By the power of truth, the power of prayer, and the power of the Holy Ghost. Here is *the truth of God*, presenting the thoughts and affections of the infinite to the finite, and opening that exhaustless storehouse of motives so wondrously suited to man's intellectual, moral, and sensitive nature. Here is *the Spirit of all grace*, without which truth is powerless, and with which it receives the welcome of the warm affections, is enthroned in the chambers of the inner man, and sanctifies and saves. Here, too, is that heaven-ordained *spirit of grace and supplication*, setting in motion all other instruments and agencies, and demonstrating man's impotence, and God's faithfulness as a prayer-hearing God.

We may not speak loosely when we speak of this moral influence of the sanctuary. It is not the mere form of godliness it would secure, but the power; it is not names, but things; it is not the shadow, but the substance. Pagan ablutions, and papal crosses and sprinklings, are not piety. The ostentation of religious observances, and the decencies of a visible morality, are sometimes found among the scoffers at all heart-religion. A Christian creed and a Christian profession are not unknown among those who are dead in trespasses and sins. Inspect the fruits of the sanctuary, and it will be found that it is the rain of heaven and the Sun of righteousness by which they are matured, and the hand of the sanctifier that gathers them. Holiness has taken the place of sin, gladness the the place of sorrow, light of darkness, hope of despair, life of death, where the sanctuary is clothed with power. Nor do we hesitate to say that, various as are the means by which the world is converted to God, and beautifully coöperative as they are, the pivot on which the machinery rests, the main shaft that impels it, its motive power, is the fire on God's altars. To this hallowed spot the church militant and the church triumphant look with hope, and here from under the sanctuary the waters issue that give life to the world. The very walls of the sanctuary are monitors, and the entrance in at the doors reads the lesson, "This is the way, walk ye in it." There is no safer path, nor is is there a more effective repulse to the Tempter than to say to him, *I am going to the house of God.*

I love to look at the sanctuary in the retired village or the crowded city; in the bold foreground, or the retreating shadows of the distant landscape. It is God's vineyard, where " the vine flourishes, and the tender grape appears," while around its consecrated walls is " God's acre," where the plants of righteousness, thickly set and deep, are gathering their immortal bloom. The beauties of holiness and the glories of immortality are there. Yes, I love to look at such a scene, and to say when I look at it, " How goodly are thy tents, O Jacob, and thy tabernacles, O Israel; as valleys are they spread forth, as gardens by the river's side, as lignaloes which the Lord hath planted, and as cedar trees beside the waters?" The dewy eve, the blushing morn, fade in comparison with this garden of God, sparkling in the beauties of holiness, and fragrant with its sweet perfume. Bashan languisheth, and the flower of Lebanon languisheth: holiness never withers; its leaf is green even in the year of drought. Glorious beyond all but the foretelling pen of prophecy, are the bright destinies of the sanctuary: glorious to feel and enjoy, glorious to *behold*, and, in seasons of darkness and despondency, glorious to look for. When that hope is realized, then will be the jubilee of the world. The ingathering of the great harvest year shall have come, when the "plowman shall overtake the reaper, and the treader of grapes him that soweth seed, and the mountains drop down sweet wine, and all the hills do melt." Intimately connected with these thoughts,

III. There is a third reason for this religious reverence for the sanctuary, and that is **its ACTIVE BENEVOLENCE.**

The church of God, from its origin and organization, from the laws by which it is governed, and the profession and character of its members, from the peculiar privileges it enjoys and the means of its advancement, from its opportunities for usefulness, and the promised favor of its Great Head, possesses notoriety and preëminence. She is like a city set on a hill, which cannot be hid. While generation after generation has passed away, and thrones **and** dynasties have vanished, and proud institutions have crumbled to the dust, and every ancient work of man is lost, this great work of God remains—a living community in a dying world, a spiritual community, youthful and vigorous, where all things else grow old and decay.

God's sanctuary is everywhere invested with this commanding position, in order to impose upon it the obligations of active service: "To whom much is given, of him also much shall be required." Its mission is to "do good and communicate." It is not erected to be looked at and admired, but to speak **to** us, to act upon us. Its province and its office are to send out its sympathies to the ignorant, and enlighten them; the wandering, and reclaim **them;** the lost, and save them. We hold of very little account that cold and dead orthodoxy which paralyzes effort. The professed Christian, who folds his hands and congratulates himself that he has nothing **to do for a** world that lieth in wickedness, because *believing* is his business, and not *working*, **is in** nothing better than the slothful servant. An enlightened belief in the doctrines of grace, so far from diminishing Christian diligence, impels **to** it by superadded obligations and motives. Our obligations to holiness and **to every form of active service, are** just as real **and just** as binding as they would have **been** had the Saviour **never** fulfilled all righteousness; just as real and just as binding as they would have been had we been justified by the deeds of the law. If salvation is *of* grace, it is *unto* works; we are fellow-workers with God. **He** works in us that we may work. We look to him as though he did all, and we labor as though all the work were our own. We have this treasure in earthen vessels, that the excellency of the power may be all of God and not of us; yet do "we strive mightily, according to the grace that worketh in us mightily." Nor is this coöperation the less obvious and delightful because our agency is human and divine. It is "the worm Jacob" that is to "thresh the mountains, and beat them small, and make the hills as chaff."

Such is the creed of the sanctuary, and with this it stands in the midst of a perishing world. None are overlooked by it, old or young, far off or near. Emphatically are *the young* its charge, because God has committed them to it; it is the sanctuary that modifies and moulds their character. It has a larger heart, too, and a more enlarged vision than this. It looks over this sin-struck earth, and cares for the heathen at home and the heathen abroad. Its thoughts, its counsels, its prayers, its gifts, its deeds of self-denial and endurance, form no inconsiderable part of the history of the church of God.

You wonder, perhaps, that I utter such obvious truths; not only would I utter, but enforce them. If God requires it of his ministers that they be working men, he also requires it of his churches that they be working churches. What kind of a light would that be that does not shine, or what sort of a church is that which has no forthgoing activity? What is Christianity without the benevolent deeds which Christianity produces? We do not ask what the sanctuary *is*, so much as what the sanctuary *does*. There may be a dead sanctuary, as well as a dead faith. A dead sanctuary? what is it? There is no heart there, and no active pulsations; it is no living temple; it is *Death!* If it acts not, it lives not; its sublimest devotions are but sounding brass and a tinkling cymbal, without **its** active character. If *this* edifice is worthy the place it occupies, and the cause to which we devote it, we must have an honest and an earnest Christianity, permeated with more of the popular element, employing more heads, more hearts, and more hands. We must have a willing people, and lay under contribution every tribe, every family, every man. This is what sanctuaries are built for. They are not built for the minister, but for the people. The minister is nor the church, nor is the pulpit the sanctuary. It is the solitude of his toil that is very apt to dishearten even the most courageous **laborer.** The difference between a ministry standing alone **and a** ministry upheld and encouraged by the favor **and** coöperation of an effective church, cannot be known this side eternity. Negligence is the sin of Christians, and it is no small sin. The want of well-doing is one of the devil's forms of evil-doing. The Saviour's maxim was, "I must *work*." I must "work the work **of** him that sent me while it is day; the night cometh, in which no man can work." We cannot prolong the day of labor an hour. Time does not wait for our indecision, nor death for our delay. It would be a lamentable narrative hereafter **to** be told, that the generation which is now passing through this house of God has left no luminous track behind it.

Nor let it be thought that **we** derogate from the dignity and sacredness of our subject, when **we** remark—

IV. In the fourth place, that the sanctuary is distinguished for its CONSERVATIVE PRINCIPLES.

It is no enemy to reform and progress; yet is it no part of its principles or its policy to "**do evil that good may come.**" It hails every aggressive movement on the kingdom of darkness; yet it **is** not heedless of consequences. Reform **and** progress are its great object; yet it has no organ of destructiveness. While it is not blind to existing evils, **it** dreads the evils of premature reform. So long as it acts in its true character, its aim is to make the world wiser, better, and happier; nor will its work be accomplished until "the Lord God shall cause righteousness and praise to spring forth before all nations." Yet it does not run riot, **even in** advancing the right and eradicating the **wrong, lest by** ill-timed and unhallowed zeal **it should lose more than it would gain.**

If the world in which we dwell is **so** impregnate with wickedness that it cannot endure the teachings of heavenly wisdom without secret hostility or open turbulence, we may not forget that the bitterness, the turmoil, the angry invective and strife **of** the world, belong not to the house of God. It is no friend to rancor and bitterness, even in a good **cause.** We accord to **it,** nay, we claim for it, its controversy with evil; and it is a controversy which is uncompromising. But we see not why it may **not** breast itself in the very front of the battle, without "scattering firebrands, arrows, and death." It is not the fiery meteor, but rather is it like the moon, wading in her brightness through a night of storms. Embarrassing, obscuring clouds it may look for, but it shines by its own light, pure and white, though making its way through Egyptian darkness. It is no thunder-cloud, filling the hearts of men with fear; nor, when its seals are opened, **do** the stars of heaven fall to the earth as a fig-tree casteth her untimely figs. No, no! Soft and gentle breezes blow from Mount Zion; **the Sun of** righteousness lingers upon its summit, and bright **visions** open upon the vale below.

The longer I live, the more I am convinced that this is one of the great characteristics of the sanctuary. It was not the earthquake, nor the strong wind, nor the fire, that made the prophet wrap his face in his mantle, but the still, small voice.

We forget our office when we needlessly ignite and inflame the worst passions of the human heart, and strike blow after blow upon the foundations of **pu**blic tranquillity. The great statute-book of the sanctuary is a cautious instructor, enforcing its lessons with "the meekness of wisdom." There is much that it teaches, and some truth which it does **not** teach; wisely leaving the great principles it inculcates, like the leaven hid in three measures of meal, to their quiet and progressive power. If the Apostle Paul could have had the private ear of Nero, I have no doubt he would have told him truths which the Spirit of God would not allow him publicly to declare to the Christians at Rome. His object was, not to agitate and revolutionize, but to regenerate and reform. Sudden changes in the polity and affairs of the world the sanctuary does not look for. It aims, not so much at rudely undermining old institutions, and demolishing old landmarks, as at leaving them silently and gradually to crumble and wither under the subduing power of truth and love. A few wild and unseasonable blasts of the trumpet may produce a storm which even the "Sermon on the Mount," a thousand times repeated, cannot assuage. There is no such reforming power as the cross of Christ. And the beauty of the reform is, that it is accomplished without doing any harm. When the sanctuary concentrates the energy of its intellect, the ardor of its emotions, and its fiery zeal, in a prolonged crusade against some one social evil, it is very apt to lose sight of its appropriate work, to exhaust its vigor in a foreign service, and, in the end of its eccentric course, take up the lamentation, "They made me keeper of the vineyards, but my own vineyard have I not kept."

Our own land stands first and foremost of all

lands in the unshackled influence of the sanctuary. For his religious principles no man is here accountable but to his Maker. The church has no jealousy of the state, and the state has no jealousy of the church. We have no inmingling of the cross and the clay. There is no ecclesiastical domination to dictate the measures of the government, and "no Star Chamber to trample the rights of conscience under the heel of arbitrary power." Our obligations, therefore, *as American churches*, stand abreast with our high privileges. In a land where the people influence the government, rather than the government the people; where public opinion originates the laws; where the church can prosper without the state, better than the state without the church; and where the religion of the gospel stands confessed as the only bulwark of national security, the sanctuary has obligations of no ordinary kind. Our free institutions do not adhere to our soil or climate, nor do our rich prairies nourish them, nor are they imbedded in our mountains; they rest on the influence of the sanctuary. Selfish politicians, noisy patriots, and profligate courtiers, are not for the state to lean upon. Our prosperity, OUR UNION, is inseparable from our Christian character. The severe schooling and steady habits of our fathers laid the foundation of our greatness, and it has thus far been protected and sustained by the laws of that kingdom which is not of this world. What the future will be, we know not; if we have fears, it is because we have fears for the influence of the sanctuary; and if we have more and stronger hopes than fears, it is because the sanctuary is his abode who "ruleth the raging of the sea, and stilleth the tumult of the people." Mercurial and fiery spirits may find a place within its walls, and threatening voices and mighty thunderings may agitate it; but there are words of peace above the howlings of the storm. If a bright horizon is yet to open upon us; if "young America," with her headstrong impulsiveness, is preserved from the turbulence of anarchy; if, in the murky atmosphere that now and then envelops us, and if, amid the hoarse and sharp rumbling of the cavern beneath us, we avoid or survive the earthquake, it will be because "knowledge, with strength of salvation, is the stability of our times."

If it so happens that we live in an age when these thoughts are unwelcome, or are looked upon with suspicion, or will be misinterpreted and abused, the more is the pity, and the more is the need of them. Well assured am I that the time will come when they will receive a hearty response from all right-hearted men, and that experience will show that "wisdom is justified of her children." We ask for this house of God that it may be baptized with the spirit of wisdom, and long remain as God's witness to whatsoever things are lovely, whatsoever things are true, whatsoever things are pure, whatsoever things are honest, whatsoever things are **of good report.** Should the time ever come when it ceases to **be the** reprover of wickedness, and at **the** same time the patron of good order, some weeping prophet **may** survey its ruins and say, "How is the gold become dim, and the most fine gold changed!" Give us this spiritual, this conservative character, and our "walls will be salvation **and** our gates praise."

V. We reverence the sanctuary, in **the** last **place,** for ITS SOCIAL AND FRATERNAL CHARACTER.

There **is but one true religion in the universe.** The **religion of heaven and the religion of earth, varying as they do in** measure, are **in their nature essentially** the same.

The sanctuary **is the house of** prayer *for all people.* It is the **symbol of** man's brotherhood, and stands forth as the sacred asylum of *fallen humanity.* So far from being appointed for **one** nation, one **clime, one** class, **or** color, it recognizes **no** distinction **of names** or persons, and **no covenant** of peculiarity. **Of all places in the world,** it is **the place where Jew and Gentile, rich and poor, bond** and free, wise and unwise, seamen and landsmen, the stranger and the home-born, are regarded with a Christian impartiality. And why should it not be so? They are alike the offspring of the same Almighty Parent; invested with the same intelligent and immortal existence; subjects of the same moral government; equally the heirs of sin and the curse, and the offered salvation; all born to trouble, as the sparks fly upward; all destined to lie down in the grave, to stand at the bar of the final judge, and, as they employ this day of grace, to be at last associated in the same blessed heaven, or in the same awful hell.

All have a common interest, therefore, in the house of God. Attractive it may be to the rich, but never ought to be repulsive to the poor. One of its peculiarities is, that "the rich and the poor meet together" at its altars. It speaks to all: to the peasant in his hut, and to the king on his throne; to the saint in his closet, and to the criminal in his dungeon; to the children of want and woe everywhere. It is the great leveller; not by obliterating all human distinctions, but by making a distinction that absorbs them all; not by depressing the high, but by elevating the low, and raising both to the dignity of "the sons and daughters of the Lord God Amighty."

Man is a social being; his religious privileges, and obligations, and hopes, are intimately inwoven with this great element of his nature. Most beautifully and wonderfully are the social relations made subservient to his immortality. Christian churches are not more certainly the nurseries of the church in heaven, than Christian families are the nurseries of the church on earth. If you survey the lands where God's altars are thrown down, or have never been erected, you will be apt to find them lands where the social and domestic ties are sacrificed to those that are more public; where the endearments of private life are usurped by a proud ambition, and the allurements to personal piety are lost in the clamor and bustle of the world. "Come, thou and *all thy house*, into the ark;" this is the voice which issues from the sanctuary of God. Our attachments to the sanctuary may well be expressive of our attachment to the worship and the God of our fathers; and well may they be strengthened by the sweet memories of the domestic circle. I would not part with these sacred reminiscences. Oh! how sweetly they sometimes come back upon us in the days of pensiveness and grief; and when we stand in silence over the honored grave of the departed; and where, amid the many bonds that united us, none is more valued than that which bound us to the house of God. We honor the solitary chamber where grief is bathed in tears, and the mourner takes refuge by himself in the bosom of eternal love; but it is not as when assembled Israel, in the day of their rebuke, bowed together in heaviness at the evening sacrifice. We sympathize with the publican when he went up alone to the temple to pray; but it is a most cheering scene to look at, which the Psalmist speaks of, when he says, "We took sweet counsel together, and went to the house of God in company." There is beauty and forth-going praise in the lonely star that twinkles in the retiring **cloud**; but it falls short of the beauty of **the** spangled heavens, nor is it the adoring anthem when "the morning stars *sang together*, and *all* the **sons** of God shouted for joy."

And may we not extend these **thoughts to the** great brotherhood of churches of every **name?** Christian men are Christian men everywhere. Though they have **been** dispersed through different ages of time, and **are** now dispersed through different sections of the church of God, they are the same Christian men everywhere. Though they differ in their intellectual endowments and acquisitions, and even in their spiritual character, **joys, and influences, they are** still good and Christian men. **Like scattered rays of light and love, they all radiate from** God's sanctuary. Their religion **is one; they** themselves are constituent parts of the one body of which Christ is the head; one temple, of which **he** is the Deity; **one** sphere, of which he is the Sun.

Whence, then, this **moral chaos?** Why this scattering of the one fold **of** the great Shepherd? Whence is it that the old faith and the old char**ity** are separated by almost impassable barriers?

Why this "party-colored blazonry," and this "cross firing of the hosts marshalled under the Captain of our salvation? We plead for God's sanctuary; **and, on** its behalf, we ask for what we have ever given, and hold ourselves ready to give—the interchanged tokens of love and influence, which the Bible not only justifies but demands. That Book of God has its standard of church-fellowship, and here it is: "Grace be with all them that love our Lord Jesus Christ in sincerity!" Here it is still more definitely: "In Christ Jesus neither circumcision availeth anything, nor uncircumcision, but a new creature. And as many as walk ACCORDING TO THIS RULE, peace be on them, **and mercy upon** the Israel of God!" Here it is again, in the words of our loving Master: "Father, I pray that *they all may be one*, as thou, Father, art in me, and I in thee, that they may be one in us, *that the world may* believe that thou hast sent me!" Who can stand before such an appeal as this? Where is now the stern Anabaptist, and the unyielding pretender to apostolic succession, and the sturdy champion of the exclusive divine right of Presbytery, and the devout advocate for the literal version of the Psalms of David, who of such figments would erect a wall of brass around the sanctuary?

We have no desire to be regarded as "uncommon pretenders to charity." Ye are our witnesses that we are not slow in "contending earnestly for the faith once delivered to the saints." Yet we have no war, except with error and sin; and where the error is radical to the Christian system, or essential to the Christian character, it is a war of extermination. But we have long since learned that conformity is not essential to unity, nor to Christian fellowship. "The kingdom of God is not meat and drink, but righteousness, and peace, and joy in the Holy Ghost." The more the faith and fellowship of Christ prevail, the more will they lead his followers to fellowship with each other. The sanctuary calls upon us to receive and acknowledge all Christians, of every name, who are Christians indeed. Oh! we are sick at heart of this dismembered body of Christ! Nor do we mean in this matter to be fettered by sectarian intolerance, or awed by the authority of men. Blessed be God, the time is coming when the "watchmen shall see eye to eye, and lift up their voice together, and with the voice together shall they sing." We look for such a day, and on this side the heavenly world. And what a beautiful expression of the object and design of the sanctuary and of the spirit of heaven! The sanctuary below is but the vestibule to the sanctuary above. We would not come to it, feeling that we are dissociated from any one of the families of the redeemed, any more than we are dissociated from "the house not made with hands, eternal in the heavens." There the earthly sanctuary terminates in the companionship of "an innumerable company of angels, and the spirits of just men made perfect, and God, the Judge of all, and Jesus, the Mediator of the new covenant."

Such is God's sanctuary. Who can appreciate it ?—its object, its toil, its solicitudes and discouragements, its expectations and successes, its honors and rewards; what is there on the earth to be compared with these ? In its moral power and permanent influence it stands preëminent above the forum, above the senate-house, above the battle-field, and above the press. Thought looks to it for instruction ; the wounded conscience looks to it as its refuge, and the burdened heart for its repose. Lisping childhood looks to it, and buoyant youth, and vigorous manhood, and hoary age. Christianity looks to it as its defender, and as the heaven-designated herald of its glad tidings. The history of the sanctuary would be the history of Christianity in all its lights and shadows, in all its depression and triumph, in all its conflicts and victories. Nations live or die, as their sanctuaries rise or fall. Woe to the land that is not the land of the Sabbath and the sanctuary ! All the world over, with the exception of those temples where God once dwelt, and from which his glory is departed, an intimate sympathy will be found to exist between the sanctuary and the best interests of men. If Scotland, from having been "one of the rudest, one of the poorest, one of the most turbulent countries in Europe," has become "one of the most virtuous, one of the most highly civilized, one of the most flourishing, one of the most tranquil," it is because "He that dwells between the cherubim there shines forth."

When a body of Puritans in the North of England, and after them a body of the "Scotch-Irish," removed to this western wilderness, in order to enjoy liberty of conscience, their rallying-point was the house of God. And now, like a wreath of perennial flowers, everywhere adorning hill and valley, their scattered temples are inmingling their hallowed incense with the winds of our mountains and the spray of our iron-bound coast. A right-minded foreigner can hardly pass through the length and breadth of this land without observing that one of our strong peculiarities is a religious reverence for God's sanctuary. What citadels of strength are these unnumbered Christian temples, everywhere lifting their spires toward heaven! Should ever the time come when a barbarous deluge, like that which inundated the fairest portions of Europe during the middle ages, passes over this land, among its first and most ruthless desolations would be found a desecrated or a desolated sanctuary.

These thoughts give interest to this welcome hour. While the tide of life has been sweeping away the landmarks of the past, some few remain who saw our ancient sanctuary in its glory, and still more who witnessed its decay. Thanks to God, the overflowing waters have thus far been restrained from invading these altars. We have lived to see the top stone of this edifice laid, and its doors open to us. We have nothing to ask for in the external and material arrangements of this house. It is not a gorgeous edifice; it has no decorated walls and arches, and no splendid magnificence. Yet are there stability and comfort, and tasteful architecture, which do honor to the genius and fidelity of those employed in projecting, erecting, and embellishing it. "*Strength* and *beauty* are in his sanctuary." We have sufficient interest and sufficient gratification in the external and the material; God grant that **we** may have a deeper feeling for the internal and the spiritual! Why should the visible captivate us, and the lust of the eye and the pride of life charm our hearts to those things that are seen, instead of attracting them to the unseen realities, of which these symbols, these appearances, are only the shadow.

The sanctuary is more than ornamental architecture, and harmonious music, and external worship. We look above and across the visible, to Him who is invisible. It is the selected spot where the Almighty architect forms the materials of "the living temple, built up with lively stones, an holy temple in the Lord, an habitation of **God through the Spirit.**" It is God's house, and we come to dedicate it to him. And there is, in my humble judgment, no superstition, but great propriety and truth in these acts of dedication. There is, and there ought to be, as wide a distinction be**tween the house** of God and all other places of public resort, as between all that is secular and all **that is sacred.** The one is a select and consecrated **territory; the other** belongs to the business of the world. Secular themes and secular objects have their place, **but that** place is not the sanctuary. From our hearts we dedicate this edifice to **the** God of heaven. It is nothing to us if he do not occupy it. STAND UP, all ye people, and before God, angels, and men, consecrate it to his worship and honor, to whom it belongs!—each one of us **humbly** looking to him, that he would fill it with **his great glory.** Be it ever sacred to him by whose **name it is** called!—sacred to his mercy-seat and his **praise!**—sacred to his **pure gospel, to his own** ordinances, **to the** fellowship of the saints, **the conversion** of men, and the comfort and edification of those who fear God and love his Son. Sacred place! "Arise, O Lord God, thou and the ark of thy strength! Let thy priests be clothed with righteousness; and let thy saints shout for joy!" From this good hour let this house be devoted only to sacred and religious uses. Here let all that is sacred be put in motion, and all that is secular be put at rest. In his name, to whom we have thus solemnly dedicated it, we say to you, Reverence God's sanctuary. Prize his ordinances, and teach your children to prize them. There are fountains of mercy here; a river the streams whereof make glad the city of our God, the holy place of the tabernacles of the Most High. Bend over this living fountain and drink to the full. Lift up your hands in the sanctuary and *bless the Lord.* The Lord, that made heaven and earth, *bless thee* out of Zion.

It will not be looked for, on the present occasion, that I should repeat those historical notices that were given in the *last discourse* that was delivered in our former edifice. It is natural for those who are in an advanced period of life to look forward; Christianity looks forward with hope. "The Brick Presbyterian church in the city of New York" will not, we trust, prove recreant to its character nor its trust. There have been periods when we have had some misgivings as to the course this church has pursued; yet, upon a deliberate review of it, it is our welcome conviction that, under the divine favor, the true purpose of the sanctuary, notwithstanding all our imperfections, has been here, in some good measure, accomplished. When we look at the number and standing of those ministers of the gospel whom its prayers and its bounty have sent forth to the world; when we advert to the part it has taken in organizing some, and in sustaining other institutions for the spread of the gospel; when we think of the multitudes to whom the gospel has been here preached, and the multitudes who hail from this church as their spiritual birthplace; when we recall its conflicts with error and its conservative influence; when we set before our minds the two generations of the Lord's people who have gone from us to the upper sanctuary, and dwell with such gratified emotions upon the scenes of trial through which they passed, and upon their peaceful departure; and when, in our present survey of this people, we count so few among this adult population who have not named the name of Christ, we bow our knees in humility and thankfulness before the God and Father of our Lord Jesus Christ, that, much as we have to deplore, we have not run in vain, neither labored in vain; "yet not I, but the grace of God that was with me."

We enter upon our new career under few circumstances of discouragement, and many of bright anticipation. We are at a sufficient remove from our sister churches to forbid all interference or rivalship, while we are in the midst of a population that give us welcome, and bid us God speed. With no ordinary gratification, also, we greet the return to our number of so many of those who, because the place has been too strait for us, have for a short season been the adornment of other and more convenient churches. We need them, and **here,** we trust, they will once more find themselves at home.

In the name of the Lord, therefore, we set up our banners. It is an eventful age of the world in which our enterprise receives this new impulse. They are cheering scenes we look upon, as from this mount of vision and this hour of hope we look down on the ages of mercy that already begin to visit our guilty world. Even now is the "earth helping the woman." The halls of science, the inventions of art, the resources of commerce, and, above all these, the facilities of **international** intercourse, are becoming tributary to Him in whom all nations shall be blessed, and even the battle of the warrior has prepared the way for the Prince of Peace. More than all, the ever-blessed and adorable Spirit of God is coming forth to the bright conquests of the "latter-day glory." The crisis is approaching, and startling events may be looked for in the future history both of the church and the world. Nor may you be dismayed, my brethren, if mercy and judgment still stand abreast in the redemption of men. If the spirit that now worketh in the children of disobedience is gone up with his legions on the length and breadth of the earth, it is but to herald his own overthrow, and be the precursor of "quietness and assurance forever." A few fleeting centuries, and the work of the sanctuary will be accomplished, and the church militant enjoy her repose.

I have before made the remark, that I did not favor the removal which we have lived to witness, **from** personal considerations, for it must be clear that the small remnant of my ministry would have **been less** precarious and less toilsome had the removal never have been effected. As Israel said to Joseph, I now say to you, "Behold, *I die;* but God shall be *with you.*" Yet while I live, I ask no greater joy than to preach the gospel to this people. It would be no grief of heart to me to die on the harvest field. I would die in the midst of you, and hope that the grandchildren of those whom I have attended to their graves, will give me a resting-place, ever quiet and "Ever Green," amid their fathers' sepulchres, and where so many **sheaves have been gathered in** fully ripe from this field of labor. Nor have I **anything more to ask for this house, than** that the God of Zion would here record his name, and that among the glorious things that shall be spoken of this city of our God, **it may** be said that "this and that man **was born in** her, and that the **Highest** himself hath established her." May we not, my brethren, this day **offer** the prayer, and indeed cherish the hope, the **confidence, that "the glory of this** latter house shall be greater than that of the former"? Long may this sanctuary stand upon this holy hill, as God's witness to the favored city and land where we dwell! Here may successive generations begin their everlasting song, and your living and dying prayer and mine be, "Peace be within thy walls, and prosperity within thy palaces!" And when the last trumpet shall shake all things earthly, may every living stone of this spiritual temple bear yonder immortal inscription, "HOLINESS TO THE LORD!" How sweet the thought that, worms and sinners as we are, we ourselves may then exemplify truth, "Behold, what hath God wrought!" and in that far-off land where the Lord is the light thereof, and the Lamb its glory, our voices, with those of the loved and venerated who have gone before us, shall swell the chorus, "Blessing, and honor, and glory, and power be unto Him that sitteth upon the throne, and to the Lamb, forever!" Amen!

REDEMPTION GOD'S GREATEST WORK.

A DISCOURSE;

DELIVERED ON THE **FIFTIETH** ANNIVERSARY **OF THE AUTHOR'S**
ORDINATION AND HIS INSTALLATION AS **PASTOR OF**
THE BRICK PRESBYTERIAN CHURCH **IN THE**
CITY OF NEW YORK.

BY GARDINER SPRING.

In submitting this discourse to the public, the author may be allowed to say, that it is from the first **and** original manuscript. The transcript of it, prepared with care, **more** compact, and designed **for** the press, was consumed by fire in the office of the **printer.** I could not recollect it, and am constrained to fall **back upon** the original and very imperfect **manuscript.**   G. S.

REDEMPTION GOD'S GREATEST WORK.

"That I may plant the heavens, and lay the foundations of the earth, and say unto Zion, Thou art my people."—ISAIAH li. 16.

I HAVE selected this text as the subject of the present discourse, not because on such an occasion I shall attempt to do justice to it, but for the outlines of truth it furnishes in this retrospect of my ministry among you.

There is nothing contingent in the arrangements of the eternal Mind. The God only wise thought of everything beforehand: all was comprised in the counsel of his own will. It was a far-reaching view presented to the prophet's eye, in the beautiful chapter which contains the text. The revealing Spirit had assured him that the "Lord shall comfort Zion, and make her wilderness like Eden;" that notwithstanding the hostility of her enemies, she need not "fear the reproach of men, neither be afraid of their revilings:" and that, "though the heavens shall vanish like smoke, and the earth shall wax old like a garment, God's righteousness shall be forever, and his salvation from generation to generation." At length, summing up the whole series of promises in her complete redemption, and bringing these luminous assurances to a still brighter focus, he forges the last link in his argument by the declaration, "I am the Lord thy God, that divided the sea, whose waves roared; Jehovah of hosts is his name. And I have put my words in thy mouth, and have covered thee with the shadow of my hand, THAT I MAY PLANT THE HEAVENS, AND LAY THE FOUNDATIONS OF THE EARTH, AND SAY UNTO ZION, THOU ART MY PEOPLE." The position I desire at least, and shall attempt to illustrate, from this comprehensive declaration, is, that THE WORK OF REDEMPTION IS GOD'S GREATEST WORK.

THE FIRST THOUGHT which illustrates its greatness is the SPIRITUAL AND IMMORTAL NATURE OF ITS SUBJECTS.

The Saviour once said, "What shall it profit a man, if he gain the *whole world*, and lose his *own soul?*" Suns and planets and fixed stars are like a drop of a bucket, and vanish from our thoughts in comparison with the intellectual faculties, the moral character, and the deathless destiny of man. All that constitutes this terraqueous globe—all, all are bubbles, atoms, the very "vanity of vanities," compared with the immortal soul. Yet this is it,—this soul of man,—which is the selected subject of this redemption.

There is gradation in the works of God. The narrative which records them is one of progress and development, from unorganized matter to the organic forms of life; from the vegetable and animal to the intellectual; from the intellectual to the moral and immortal. This visible and exterior universe is a work by itself, but not for itself; everywhere indicating the divine wisdom, power, and goodness. But with all their magnificence and beauty, all their symmetry and organization, they are mere masses of inert, unconscious matter. Wondrous existences are they, and the more wondrous as the researches of science make them known to us; yet are they without sensation, without thought, without will or emotion, without the capacity of enjoyment, without enlargement and expansion. Yonder sun and moon, those planets and that milky way, and all beyond them, are now what they always were. The brightest of them all has no immortality, and in a few revolving centuries will wax old as a garment and be turned to ashes. A reflecting man at once perceives that this material creation is not the fit subject for any great and ultimate procedure of the infinite Mind. It is, and ever must be, wanting in those elements which are essential to great and lasting results.

The distinctive feature of the work of redemption is, that it rises above and beyond the objects of time and sense, and concerns itself with the immaterial, the moral, the immortal—realities that have more than a relative and temporary value, and that remain and stand fast when this external machinery of nature is broken up, and blazing planets die—realities forever enlarging, expanding forever in holiness and joy never yet attained by the loftiest seraph, or in wickedness and woe never yet endured by the foulest fiend. There are heights and depths in this onward career which imagination cannot fathom. Man's redemption alone stands abreast with his immortality, ever onward, without measure and without end. It is a new world this redemption stands related to; a new heavens and a new earth, where immortal faculties flourish, and thoughts and affections and responsibilities and joys follow the march of eternity.

In this earth on which we dwell material things are very apt to shut out the immaterial. The conflict is between the visible and the invisible, the mortal and the immortal, the sensual and the spiritual. The most distinguished naturalist of the age has expressed the opinion that those who are most devoted to the researches of natural science are most exposed to atheism. Doubting, first the reality of the immaterial world as distinct from material organization, men at length stop at second causes, and lose sight of the great First Cause. Their higher and immortal nature does not interest them. Yet is this the key-stone in the arch of the spiritual temple. Redemption rises above creation and providence by the moral and immortal nature of its subjects. These relations to eternity give it its immeasurable importance. If there are wonders in a leaf of the forest, in a beam of light, and a drop of water, what a world of wonders is man—man fallen—man redeemed—man glorified! Were the material universe crowded and compact together within the compass of the earth on which we dwell, and all its orbs of light were there, and all its hoary-headed mountains, and all its rivers, and all its palaces and gold,—one creature of God, fallen and redeemed, would outweigh them all. And if "*one* sinner that repenteth" is the joy of the holy universe, well may reason be confounded, and imagination wearied in the flight, when from the summit of Mount Zion they survey the "great multitude which no man can number," all born for immortality, that are comprised in this redemption. We need to be inhabitants of eternity, in order to appreciate the work so conversant with eternity. We look to the Cross, to learn the worth of the soul; and we look to the soul, to know the worth of the Cross. If there is no redemption, immortality is a curse; if there is no immortality, redemption is a dream. Man is worthless, if Christ is worthless. If man is more than a vain show, a worthless bubble, a sigh, a grave; if his existence, if the countless existences of humanity leap over all the landmarks of time, and roll onward to a boundless eternity, then Christ and his redemption are everything.

Look now, in *the second place*, at the MEANS BY *which his redemption is accomplished.*

These millions born for immortality, multiplied **like the** leaves of the forest and like the sand on the shore, are all fallen by their iniquity, and are the children of wrath. Sin has made the earth where they dwell a charnel-house. The dead are there. It is the cemetery of ages. The pall of midnight rests upon it. It performs its revolutions under the curse of a violated law. An impenetrable cloud hangs over it that is surcharged with wrath. How to rescue them and restore them to the divine favor, without the subversion of that righteous empire so wisely and benevolently established throughout the universe, and without a complete prostration of that justice and judgment which are **the habi**tation of God's throne, was the great prob**lem which** agitated unsearchable Wisdom to its depths. It could not be solved by an act of arbitrary power, **for** then the sovereignty of God would come in collision with his rectitude. It could not be solved by the overflowing tenderness which recoils from the execution of a law which heaven and earth pronounce holy, just, and good, but rather by some procedure which magnifies the law and makes it honorable; which vindicates its claims, and is itself the end of the law for righteousness to every one that believeth. It was a glorious object to attain, and the heart of God was set upon it as it was never set upon any other enterprise. Nor was it set upon it in vain. The method of obtaining it stands abreast with the magnitude of the work. It was no after-thought; it was wrapt up in the manifold wisdom of God. What was it? Oh! the depth of the riches both of the wisdom and knowledge of God! It was "God manifest in the flesh, justified in the Spirit, seen of angels, preached unto the Gentiles, believed on in the world, received up into glory." This is the sum and substance of the method. The inscription stands engraven as on a pillar for luminous exhibition to the world. When the Saviour said to his disciples, "I came forth from the Father, and am come into the world; again, I leave the world and go to the Father," it was the solution of the enigma, "A little while and ye shall not see me; and again, a little while and ye shall see me." We need not marvel that they replied, "Now speakest thou plainly, and speaketh no proverb." But plain and intelligible as the declaration is, it contains things which angels desire to look into.

Of all realities, this is the most astonishing—the Seed of the woman bruising the serpent's head. He whom all the angels of God worship—he to whom thousand thousands minister, and ten thousand times ten thousand stand before him—he before whose majesty and glory they cover their faces with their wings—he who, being in the form of God, thought it not robbery to be equal with God, *taking upon him the form of a servant, and made in the likeness of men!* This great fact stands alone in the history of the universe; amid all created and uncreated things there is nothing like it. Gabriel might have become a worm; but it would have been a faint adumbration of such condescension as this. The brightest prince in the court of heaven might have put off the splendor of the upper sanctuary, and, like Babylon's degraded monarch, been driven from among his pure and uncorporeal peers to eat grass like oxen, till seven times past over him; but this were but the passing and unnoticed shadow of that low estate to which the second person in the ever blessed and adorable Godhead was subjected when he was "*made of a woman*—made under the law, that he might redeem them that were under the law." What a view is this,—the mighty God, the everlasting Father becoming one of the sons of men! Four thousand years had passed away since sin and death entered upon their devastations on this earth, when, lo! the announcement was made in heaven that the Son of God was about to put on the form of a servant: and when he laid aside his celestial robes and crown, it was a day never to be forgotten; it was the jubilee of the universe celebrated on earth, and destined to be a high anniversary even in the realms of light.

Yet this was but preliminary to the **proposed** arrangement. Thus debased, the Incarnate One took upon himself the mighty aggregate of human guilt. Holy, harmless, and undefiled, as susceptible to pain and reproach as to degradation and shame, he was a man of sorrows and acquainted with grief. Legions of holy beings hung over his pathway, but it was a sad pilgrimage. His earthly existence was unceasingly embittered; and with no alleviation to his sorrows, amid embarrassments and temptations, sufferings and a self-sacrificing submission, such as the sun had never before looked upon, he trode **his** obedient way, and trode it alone, though **abuse and** insult met him at every step. Not a **disloyal act, nor** murmuring word, nor impatient emotion, nor reluctant wish, marked his history from first to last. Dark and dismal as was the last scene, the service and the suffering had attractions for him even beyond the glory he had with the Father before the world was. He foresaw it all, yet he chose it; he felt it all, yet he did not recoil from the burden. **His** enemies challenged him to come down **from the** cross; but he could not come down till his work was accomplished. There, while worlds gazed upon the sight, gazing with immeasurable **interest, and** crowding around his cross, he made his soul an offering for sin—a spectacle to God and angels, men and devils—the satisfaction of justice and the purchase of eternal life.

These are the means by which this redemption was accomplished. Such is the groundwork of the sinner's pardon and justification. On these the whole redemption rests; a superstructure worthy of its eternal and glorious author, and resting on an imperishable foundation. The purpose of redeeming mercy had been stillborn but for this wonderful humiliation, this perfected abasement of the Son of God. This great fact, like the doctrine of man's accountableness and immortality, underlies all the truths of a supernatural revelation. Its types and prefigurations, its ceremonial and moral jurisprudence, its predictions in all their fulness, harmony, and progressive character, its doctrinal instruction, its promises and threatenings, its terms of salvation, its faith and hopes, all receive their fulfilment or derive their true import from Christ Jesus and him crucified. Like the star of Jacob, it lights up the night of ages that are past; and like the Sun of righteousness, foretold by Malachi, it pours its healing beams on the coming years of the right hand of the Most High. It is the great central fact in the universe. And if that is the greatest work of God which is the most Godlike and accomplished in the most Godlike way, there is nothing to be compared with this redemption.

In addition to this, it must not be forgotten that

it MAKES EVERYTHING ELSE SUBSERVIENT TO ITS INTERESTS **AND** ADVANCEMENT.

That cause for which God planted the heavens and laid the foundations of the earth, may well be regarded as important enough to lay under contribution every creature and every event in the universe. Such are the teachings of the Bible. In this great cause, God first and chiefly spared not his Son; and well does the apostle demand, "How shall he not with him freely give us all things." The greater includes the less. There is nothing in the works of creation nor in the works of providence which does not derive its importance and value from **the** relations it sustains, and the influence it exerts **upon** this redemption. Do we ask **for what and** for whom were all these worlds and beings made? the answer is, "All things were made BY HIM and FOR HIM." No matter what it is,—material and immaterial—visible and invisible—heaven, earth, thrones, dynasties, angels, men, devils,—this Redeemer is head over them all, and makes them all, in different measures and different ways, subservient to his high purpose of redeeming mercy. The mountain rivulet is not more tributary to the river, nor the thousand rivers to the ocean, **nor the** ocean in its turn more certainly to the clouds, the dew, the rain, than all things are tributary to the great design of his redemption. The sun rises and sets for him, or at his command it stands still upon Gibeon; and for him the moon walks in her brightness, or rests over the valley of Ajalon. The Rose of Sharon blooms to indicate his loveliness, and the Lily of the Valley to show forth his beauty. There is not a wave that lashes the shore, nor a tumultuous revolution among the people; there is not a portentous indication that makes the inhabitants of the world afraid at his tokens, nor a gladsome sign that makes the outgoings of the morning and the evening to rejoice, nor a sweeping flood, nor a year of famine, nor a battle of the warrior,—no, not one among all the physical or moral causes that act upon the character and condition of men, but acts also upon his cause and honor, and is, therefore, under the control of this Mediator-king. The earth we live upon would never have been created, never had its seasons revolved, nor its landscapes **smiled,** nor its Sabbaths visited us, nor its ministry **of reconciliation been** known, nor its glad tidings **listened to,** had it not been spread out as the selected theatre of a great redemption. Were a Christian statesman to look over the earth at the present hour, what a multitude of events would he discover that are indissolubly associated with the great interests of man's redemption! and how, in this inspection, would he have the key that unlocks many a mystery in the complicated affairs of men! And when, in some future age, the favored historian **shall** arise, as deeply imbued with the knowledge of God **as** with the researches of men, who shall look back and tell of the past, how certainly will his point of vision be the mountains of Zion, his pen dipped in Siloam's brook! If, when the foundation of the earth was laid, the morning stars sang together and all the sons of God shouted for joy, how inspiriting the view, and how rapturous the song, when in full and long retrospect this redemption asserts its honors, and it stands confessed that for this all things were made! Great or small, vast or minute, complicated or simple, full of terrors or of joy, dissociated from its relations to this redemption it is nothing, **it** was formed in vain. It is unworthy of God, because it is no part of that **one** grand, systematic, harmonious whole, of which the redemption is the fulfilment and **the glory.**

With such resources, therefore, we may, in the *fourth place*, take a glance at its CONFLICTS AND TRIUMPHS.

As head over all things to his church, the accredited Redeemer is a king and has a kingdom. When he stood at the bar of the Roman procurator, Pilate asked him, "Art thou a king then?" Jesus answered him, "For this end was I born, and for this cause came I into the world." Though born of a woman and crucified **as a malefactor,** God has exalted him as king upon his holy hill of Zion, and given him a name that is above every name; that at the name of Jesus every knee should bow, and every tongue confess that he is Lord, to the glory of God the Father.

Enemies he has on earth and in the dark world of perdition. His conflict is with sin; and however insidious and mysterious its working, and however **vast its** empire and severe its bondage, his object is accomplished only as the empire of wickedness is overthrown, and the kingdom of truth and holiness established in its place. This is his great object. His death and sacrifice, his boundless grace and mercy, and the perfected justification of those who believe in him, are but means to this great end. He foreknew and predestinated them that they might be conformed to the image he wears. He calls them, he justifies them, he glorifies them, his full blessing consisting in turning away every one of them from his iniquities.

The enterprise is worthy of its author; and the **greatness, the glory of it can** be measured only by **the** obstacles it surmounts. Its conflict with law and **justice** we have already adverted to, and its conquests over them. But it has other conflicts and other triumphs. That priceless thing, the soul **of man, was in the** gall of bitterness and the bonds of iniquity. This magnificent edifice, this spiritual temple where God once dwelt, was in ruins, its grandeur and beauty disfigured, defaced, polluted, and the abode of the foul spirits of darkness in every form. Sin was there in all its ugliness. Idle and wandering thoughts were there,—dreamy fancies, lying vanities, towering pride, absorbing selfishness, debasing lusts, malignant passions, prolific error, and that mother monster, enmity to God. And these were followed up and acted out in deeds of wickedness of varied form and enormity,—from the obscenity of idol altars, to their inhuman cruelty—from bold infidelity, to open contempt and profanation of all that is sacred—from the anarchy and confusion where every social tie is torn asunder, to the lawless riot which embitters all the ingredients of human intercourse—from the solitary blow of Cain, to the extermination of millions on the field of battle—from the licentiousness of the brothel, to the libertinism of the harem—from breaches of trust and deeds of dishonesty, to the ravaging of provinces—from the romancing of a fertile imagination, to the bearing of false witness against our neighbor—from the miserable shifts of avarice, to the desolations of the slave-trade—and from the sighing of the sick-chamber, to the overwhelming miseries that deluge the earth. Such is the devil's work and the fruit of man's apostasy.

Offensively and defensively, and with vigorous purpose and fearful success, have the powers of darkness prosecuted the war, sometimes by force and cruelty, and sometimes by delusion and falsehood. Nations have been deceived and enchained by it, and the "whole world lieth in wickedness," chained down in spiritual bondage, darkness, and death.

Yet "the messenger of the covenant," girded with truth, his feet shod with the preparation of the gospel of peace, having on the breastplate of righteousness, bearing the shield of faith, and armed with omnipotent power, though he did not anticipate a speedy, was sure of an ultimate triumph. The conflict needed such a champion. No other could restrain or subdue the foe. Philosophy could not do it: its sages were learned and eloquent, but they were pigmies in such a contest. Legislation could not do it: human laws, proud monument as they were of ancient civilization, were but as the spider's web. Science could not do it: with all its brilliant discoveries, it had no power to cure the leprosy of sin. Nor could the guilty and miserable victims liberate themselves. Darkness never yet created light; sin never yet vanquished sin. There is nothing in man to take the part of God against himself. Sin would reign supreme and uncontrolled, for all that men and means can accomplish; and forever reign, but for him who is stronger than the strong armed.

His work comprises redemption by price and redemption by power. Early the mandate went forth : "Gird thy sword upon thy thigh, O most mighty, with thy glory and thy majesty; and in thy majesty ride prosperously, because of truth and meekness and righteousness." A crown was given to him, and he went forth conquering and to conquer. Sometimes the day of vengeance is in his heart because the year of his redeemed is come; while his province and his prerogative are to draw his enemies by the cords of love as with the bands of a man. Nor are his victories the less real because they are noiseless. The Lord is not in the earthquake, nor in the strong wind, nor in the fire, but in the still, small voice. It is the excellency of power, gentle as the dew, and soft as the breathing of his love. It is his own new-creating Spirit; it is the Dove of heaven hovering over a lost world, and from his fleecy cloud distilling blessings that make Jerusalem a rejoicing and her people a joy. The God of heaven has no interest in the universe so dear to his heart as this. He himself presides over it, and conducts it to its glorious issues. It is his work, and his greatest work. "Behold," says he, "I create Jerusalem a rejoicing and her people a joy." The men of this world erect monuments in commemoration of events that mark important epochs in its history. They shout the praises of the hero who has fought their battles and achieved their victories. But here are the conflicts and victories of him who "hath on his vesture and on his thigh a name written, King of kings, and Lord of lords." If poets and painters depict the scenes where battles are fought and **victories** won, how much more memorable are the scenes where the Spirit descends, and the Captain of our salvation has fought and conquered! This was the joy set before him, when, without a smile, without a drop of consolation, he hung between heaven and earth, and all the waves and billows of God's wrath were passing over him. Well does he deserve the crown. Ride on, thou mighty Conquerer! the sceptre of thy kingdom is a right sceptre. Roll on, roll on, thou river of God, that art full of water! the wilderness and the cities are glad for thee; the villages that Kedar doth inhabit lift up their voice; let the inhabitants of the rock sing; let them shout from the top of the mountains! Let the triumph begin, "The kingdoms of this world are become the kingdoms of our Lord and his Christ, and he shall reign forever and ever."

Another testimony to the magnitude of this redemption is found in the fact that IT IS SO EXPRESSIVE OF THE GLORY OF ITS GREAT AUTHOR.

Unwasting as are the resources of joy and blessedness eternally within the great First Cause, he would not exist alone. If we inquire why he chose to give existence to creatures and worlds, we have the answer in the words, "Thou hast created all things, and for *thy pleasure* they exist and were created." What his great and ultimate end is in all that he does, is a question that lies deep at the foundation of all sound theology and true religion. Nor do we see but the one answer to this question; God himself is and must be his own end. The silence and the solitude of eternity were broken by the voice which "spake, and it was done; which commanded, and it stood fast." His perfections require eternity to unfold; and, though selfishness has no place in his nature, he does, as he ought, appreciate his own character and claims. All holiness and joy are from him, and are produced and perpetuated by the most perfect and harmonious manifestation of his own intrinsic and unchanging excellence. And because it exhibits his character in all its grandeur and loveliness, it is such a manifestation as gratifies his infinitely benevolent mind.

Followed out to their conclusions, these are great truths; but they are obvious truths. The infinite does not exist for the finite, but the finite for the infinite. Man's existence, and man's rectitude and happiness, point above and beyond himself. Measure the earth, count the stars, and people the moon and the planets; and when you have numbered them they are but atoms compared with the infinite "All in All;" themselves deriving their worth and importance from their forthgoing expression of the ineffable glory of the eternal and infinite One, "of whom, to whom, and through whom are all things." How obvious to the mind of any man but an atheist is it, that "God made all things for himself!" Who else should he make them for? Look above, beneath, around you! you see wisdom and design in all things. All that is, or ever will be, was made for God. Oh! it is a delightful thought. We would have God exalted everywhere, by all creatures, and always.

This redemption, originating in his warm and loving bosom,—what would it be if it were not so full of God? What would it be if from every page of the Bible, every bright day of the Son of man, every pulpit, every baptismal altar, every communion-table, every high-born hope of pardon and peace, every flowing stream from the river of life, and every bird of paradise that sings upon its outspreading branches, were they not vocal with the truth, "Not for your sakes do I this, saith the Lord God, be it known unto you, but for my great Name's sake?" No marvel that, on the early intimations of this great work, the morning stars sang together, and all the sons of God shouted for joy, and that with every progressive disclosure of it the angels cover their faces with their wings. Oh! it was a bright epoch in eternity that gave rise to a design thus comprehensive, thus carried into execution, thus glorious in its conflicts and triumphs, in order to rend the veil that shut out the glories of the Godhead from the view of creatures, and make him appear to mortal eyes—him the eternal, uncreated One—him first, him last, him midst, him everything.

Nature and providence, nay, the first covenant, are enveloped in clouds and darkness. There is a bright side to the cloud; but it is a cloud still, and has a mixture of obscurity compared with the glory that shines in the face of Jesus Christ. God's designs are deep and unfathomable, separated from his redeeming mercy. He himself was never truly known until he became Emmanuel. We see **him** now in some measure as he is. It is his great work we are looking at; the master device of his mighty intellect and surpassing love. **Vast and comprehensive as it is, it** is one which he **will never see** any **reason nor have any** desire to enlarge, **or** diminish, **or alter.** Here he has developed the ruling motive **of** his conduct, and solves every dark problem, and unweaves every intricate web in his providence. The highest exhibition of uncreated excellence which created beings have ever discovered, or ever will discover, is in this wonderful Redemption. Every eye is now thrown upon him, not as a withering abstraction; **not** as an existence demonstrated **by a** logical process; not as a personification **of** mere greatness and majesty, whom to contemplate only fills the mind with awe; but **as a** vivid representation of perfect rectitude and perfect goodness,—the unseen God seen by mortal eyes, heard by mortal ears, and his voice of love calling for a response from mortal hearts.

Yes, from **mortal eyes**, mortal ears, and mortal hearts. There is such a thing as the inward witness to the truths of this redemption. Good men contemplate it with delight and joy. There is so much in it of the God they love, of the Saviour who died for them, of the Spirit who sanctifies them, of the prospects and destiny of that kingdom of which they are the subjects, of the well-being of this world and of the interests of the universe, of the holiness and happiness of time and eternity, that every devout mind contemplates it with delightful and delighted admiration. When the truths and spirit of this redemption are no longer the objects of a mere intellectual perception, but are transferred to the believer's heart and experience, it is then that this wondrous procedure of heavenly wisdom and love is seen in its true glory and in all the beauty of holiness. In every instance of genuine conversion, **it is, as** it were, repeated and acted over anew. It has its counterpart in the bosom of every converted man. Its deity is there, because for the first time he is there enthroned and honored. His rectitude and justice are there. His abounding mercy is there. His omnipotence is there. His sovereignty is there. His faithfulness is there. The consummation of all his purposes, yea, his whole glory, is there, if not in full portrait, in amiable and impressive miniature, reflected from the cross, inwrought in the soul, and progressively changing the beholder from glory to glory, even as by the Spirit of the Lord. Every glimpse of the glory of God in the face of Jesus Christ, excites and gives enlargement to his brightest views and best affections. The separating wall between time and eternity is broken down; future things become present, and invisible things visible. We seem at such seasons to walk with God as Enoch walked, and to converse with him as the favored disciples did when he was transfigured before them. Moses felt this transforming power when he was in the mount with God, and his face shone with the lustre of the interview. Isaiah felt it, when in holy vision he saw this Jesus sitting upon a throne high and lifted up, and his train filled the temple. Paul felt it, when he was caught up to the third heavens; and John felt it in Patmos, when One like unto the Son of man spake with him from the midst of the golden candlesticks. Other truths are fugitive in their influence, and melt away in comparison with those inwoven with this redemption. These elevate and purify. They have led millions, and will lead millions upon millions more, to communion with the eternal Mind, and to growing conformity to heaven. By nothing is man so transformed and

God so glorified as by the practical working of this redemption; "according as it is written, he that glorieth let him glory in the Lord."

Such is this redemption; great in the spiritual and immortal nature of its subjects; in the means by which it has been effected; in the subserviency of all things to its interests and advancement; in its conflicts and triumphs, and in the progressive manifestations it furnishes of the glory of its author.

The views that have been presented suggest to us,

1. In the first place, *to put a just estimate upon our religious privileges*. There is a view in which the planet on which we dwell is a very insignificant thing compared with some of the worlds which float above us. The Psalmist once exclaimed, "When I consider the heavens which are the work of thy fingers, the moon and the stars which thou hast ordained, Lord, what is *man* that thou art mindful of him, and the son of man that thou shouldest visit him!" And there is a view in which this little world rises superior to any other part of the universe. Though not so large as some in the solar system; not so exalted as heaven nor so abject as hell, it stands midway between the prison and the throne. These material worlds above us are obedient to the ordinances of Heaven. From the heavenly bodies to the young leaf of the forest, they all obey the eternal

Lawgiver. This earth has violated the laws of its being, floated away from the high position originally assigned to it, and joined in the revolt of the fallen. It is a condemned world; it is the prisoner of justice, and under the sentence of outraged law. But though the prisoner of justice, it is the "prisoner of hope," and placed in a state of reprieve between condemnation and the executed sentence. When angels fell, they were condemned to chains of darkness, and the sentence was executed. Man sinned, and this great redemption interposed for his rescue. It brought him within the reach of salvation, and placed him under a system of instruction and discipline fitted to form his character for eternity. And now, as ever, it makes its appeals to his conscience and his heart, by truths and motives drawn from all that is binding in the divine authority, all that is persuasive in the tenderness of infinite love, and all that is powerful in the notes of the redeemed in contrast with the wailings of despair. It has its alone place under the mediatorial reign of the Son of God, under proclamation of the "glad tidings of great joy," under the light of Sabbaths, under the faithful and earnest ministrations of the sanctuary, and under the strivings of the Holy Spirit. These are privileges which involve man's dearest interests for time and eternity; privileges which will be remembered when pastors and people stand before God;

when all the nations are dead, the earth is burnt up, and the heavens are no more. They are privileges which, if rightly employed, secure to the heirs of immortality a holy and blessed inheritance beyond the grave. They are privileges which, by virtue of the believer's union to Jesus Christ, assign him a place above the angels who never fell, and a song which none can learn but those who are the redeemed from among men. Apostate as it is, this redemption gives an importance to the world in which we dwell, which belongs to no other world. It is destined to transform it, and make its wilderness like Eden, and its deserts like the garden of the Lord. It is honored and immortalized as the theatre of this wondrous work. Nor is there a son or daughter of Adam who makes its messages welcome, but is immortalized from this wondrous alliance to the incarnate Deity, and these great achievements of redeeming love. "Of Zion it shall be said, This and that man was born in her, and the highest himself shall establish her. The Lord shall count, when he writeth up the people, that this man was born there." Honored genealogy, that traces its lineage to the house of God! Earthly princes rarely boast of it. Not many mighty, not many noble, bear the armorial ensigns of the sanctuary; yet the poorest may claim them, and sparkle in his coronet who wears many crowns. This redemption stamps a value on these Christian privileges, great as the worth of the soul and the glories of eternity.

2. **This** redemption, in the second place, *magnifies the office of the Christian ministry.* This may not seem the most modest remark from lips that minister at the altar. Yet it was not egotism in the apostle Paul to "magnify his office." Nor may it be deemed presumption for him who addresses you to put a high estimate upon an office which sustains so intimate a relation to God's great work of redeeming mercy. When we say it is God's own appointment, and for the purpose of coöperating with him in carrying into execution that all-comprehensive **and** glorious work of redeeming mercy, we have said only that which God **has revealed.** It pleased God "by the foolishness of preaching to save them that believe." What higher encomium on the ministerial office than is contained in this single sentence! Well do we know that it has its trials, its solicitudes, its discouragements, its dependencies, its exposures, and above all, its tremendous responsibilities. Never is it relieved from that fearful burden, that to some we are the "savor of life unto life, and to some the savor of death unto death;" and never will it be otherwise than that, **if** we prove faithless, the blood of those who die **in** their iniquity "will be required at our hands." The fact that the piety, the intelligence, the usefulness of every church stand abreast with

the piety, the intelligence, the usefulness of their minister; that their spiritual and intellectual attainments rise and fall with his; that if he walks with God and drinks into the spirit of his divine Master, so will their hearts be filled with these glowing graces; that if his study is deserted, and his prayers and preaching become feeble, his people will become even more feeble than their minister;—all these show the magnitude of his office. Yet the thought that magnifies it most is the near relation it sustains to the great redemption of the Son of God. The privilege and blessedness of sympathizing with the High Priest of the Christian profession in his devotement to the glory of his Father; in his love for the souls of men; in his consecration to interests higher than his own; and in his expectations, honors, and reward,—these are the immunities of the sacred office. It is no ordinary privilege to be laid under the necessity of cultivating an intimacy with those revealed principles of truth and morals which lie at the foundation of the Christian system, and which are inwoven with all holy character on earth and in heaven. The business of a gospel minister is with the Bible, there to acquaint himself with the only living and true God, and Jesus Christ whom he has sent; his views the sweeter, as his faith is the more intense; the brighter, as they are the more enlarged; the more sure and undoubted, as they cordially embrace the great elements and relations of this redemption. I honor other professions; but there is no service so important, so delightful, so honorable, as to be thus associated with the great prophet of the Christian profession, in the midst of those wondrous scenes and truths and realities so intimately associated with the manifold glory of God and the progressive conquests of his reigning Son. Statesmen may envy such a service. Monarchs on their thrones are not so favored as the minister of Christ. No laurels retain their freshness like those he is permitted to entwine around the head of his divine Lord. Go, ye who minister at God's altar! go and proclaim salvation to dying men! Go, tell the weary and heavy-laden, the tempest-tost and the desponding, of him who is a hiding-place from the storm! Go, search out the mysteries of this redemption, and with every new truth illustrated, and every new subject of its transforming power, let your own heart and lips respond, "Glory to God in the highest; and on earth peace and good will to men!"

Had my own allotment been a less favored one, I hope I could say, "I thank our Lord Jesus Christ for that he counted me faithful, putting me into the ministry." Would that I had been, and were more worthy of the office; but I am more than satisfied that I am a minister of Christ. I never desired a higher station than to be the servant of the church for Jesus' sake. I ask no more of the world, nor of the church, nor of God my Saviour, if he will but make me faithful unto death, and give me a crown of life. When I think of the work itself in which I have been so long employed, I count "the laurels of a Cæsar weeds," compared with the honors of the humblest minister of the everlasting gospel. Our subject, then,

3. In the last place leads us to *a brief review of my own prolonged ministry among this people.* I have many things to say, and many which I must suppress. Fifty years ago this Sabbath I first occupied the pulpit of the Brick church as your pastor. I remember the day well; some four or five of you remember it, when, in a crowded assembly of those who now sleep in the dust of the earth, I bowed my knees before the God and Father of our Lord Jesus Christ, and received this sacred trust from him, "through the laying on of the hands of the Presbytery." To me it was a solemn day, and associated with a sense of responsibility which followed me through the whole of my ministry. The half century is gone; gone, like the dying cadence of distant minstrelsy as it vibrates into air; gone, like the phantom which in prospect had the semblance of reality, but which in the retrospect has melted away; gone, like some small star that has been twinkling on the curtain of the night; gone, like the leaves which the wind of autumn has swept

away ; gone, like clouds which vanish into air, after they have exhausted their treasures upon the land ; gone, as the word just spoken, for good or for evil, never to be recalled ; gone, as yesterday is gone :—all, all have vanished one by one into the mysterious past. Yet, short and rapid as has been the flight of these fifty years, they form an eventful period. The wheels of providence have been revolving, sometimes high and terribly, sometimes in circles bright and radiant ; while those who have been spectators of these varied scenes, only wonder at the changes which a few short years have wrought, and gratefully admire the wisdom and goodness of him who is so rapidly preparing the agencies by which the final consummation of all things is hastening on. God's plans are large and comprehensive. His great heart is set upon the fulfilment of his gracious purpose to our lost world. As we have seen, all his designs stand related to this great design ; nor is he slack concerning his promise as some men count slackness. "My Father worketh hitherto," says the Saviour, "and I work." He is the most diligent and effective worker in the universe. His eye never slumbers, and his arm is never weary. This half century bears testimony to the fitness and coöperation of those second causes, both in the material and moral creation, by which his gracious purposes are accomplished. Epochs and events there have been during its progress, which seemed at first view to be of dark augury, and which threatened to put back the shadow on the dial of time, if not to defeat the counsels of the God only wise. But the "Lord seeth not as man seeth." His work never stands still— never goes backward. ONWARD is the motto of the upper sanctuary; and as fast as infinite goodness and wisdom will admit, onward the work goes. Within these fifty years, two generations of men have passed away. They have done their work; the generation that followed them is in training for a mightier work to come. Thrones and dynasties have been demolished and overturned, and new thrones and policies established which, in defiance of the powers of darkness, contain the germs and elements of that "knowledge and strength of salvation" which are destined to be the stability of the world. Science and the arts, so long held in abeyance because the nations were not prepared to employ them to benevolent ends, we ourselves have seen making such progress as to change the face of human affairs. We have heard, indeed, and still hear of the battle of the warrior, and of garments rolled in blood; but the splendor of war has vanished. The shock of armies no longer lends its bewildering fascinations to the poet's numbers; and what is more, the storm is heralding the advent of the Prince of Peace, and sweeping away those otherwise insurmountable barriers to the propagation of the gospel among the nations. Let it be recorded with fervent gratitude, that the past fifty years have accomplished more for the extension of the gospel to the distant heathen, more for the dissemination of God's word, more for the circulation of religious truth, more for enlightening the ignorant and elevating the abject of our race, and more for the Christian occupancy of the talents God has given his church, than any ten preceding centuries. And they furnish, also, a delightful fulfilment of the promise, "He that watereth shall be watered himself." God's own Spirit has been descending on the broad lands of Christendom, pouring water upon him that is thirsty, and floods upon the dry ground.

It has been a great privilege to live in such an age as this, and emphatically so to have occupied the place of a fellow-worker with God in the prosecution of that design for which he stretched abroad the heavens, and laid the foundations of the earth. We have no confidence in human inventions for the accomplishment of the great object for which the Son of God became incarnate, and died. Philosophy, legislation, science, different forms of government, civilization, socialism, infidelity, philanthropy, have done their best to eradicate the moral diseases of our nature, and renovate this apostate world; but the highest achievements they can boast of, are some slight modifications of its symptoms, while they leave the deep-seated plague untouched. The gospel alone is the power of God and the wisdom of God, and the living ministry is his own appointed vehicle for conveying it to the minds of men. It is this which gives such unmeasured responsibility to the position I have been allowed, for so long a period, to hold among you as your unworthy pastor.

I cannot be too thankful to the Father of mercies that I was led to commence my ministry among you, under a deep impression that it it must be a ministry of incessant watchfulness and toil, and that from the outset my mind was never bewildered by day-dreams of leisure and repose in the pastoral office. Dr. Johnson once said, that "he pitied the man who made the Christian ministry an easy work." Whether or not I have made it so, and what have been my motives in laboring among you, is not for me to decide. God is witness that my work has been my joy, and most my joy when it has been most severe. I did not enter the ministry as a secular calling, but because I loved,—nay, if you will pardon me for saying it,—because I was enamored of the gospel. I did not enter it for its honor, nor for its wealth. I sought a rural charge; but God sent me among the wealthy and bountiful, who adopted me in my youth, and have not forsaken me in my old age. I was thrown among religious teachers greatly my superiors, and saw at a glance that I had everything to do if I ever became an able minister of the New Testament. I could easily dazzle my audiences, and please their imagination, and excite **their** emotions, by **a** beautiful tableau of words; but when **I** retired **to** my chamber I could not but ask myself, *What does it all amount to?* Much I had to learn, in order to understand, illustrate, and defend the truths of the gospel, and enforce its duties; and, instead of that blustering declamation which gratifies without instructing, which creates a sensation without sinking one thought into the soul, **learn to** present clear and forcible views of God's **revealed** will. **It** is not one truth merely that **a minister is** called to preach, or that the people ought to **hear,** but " **the whole** counsel of God "—**all the** truths and **all the** duties of the gospel.

To what extent the present age is in advance of the past, in consequence of its disrelish for doctrinal preaching, let the limited acquaintance with Christian truth of the great mass, even of the more intelligent laymen, bear witness. The Bible everywhere insists on **the belief** of the truth as the basis of Christian character. What men do **not believe** they cannot practise. That piety **and those active** efforts cannot long be depended **on that do not** arise from **the** love of God's truth. **Let the fire** of God's truth **be** withdrawn, and though by its own momentum the sacred machinery will move a while, it is sure to stop. Men who complain of doctrinal preaching are strangers to the worth and power of practical preaching. When I read the works of Owen and Doddridge, of Toplady and Baxter, of Howe and Charnock, of Edwards and Chalmers, of Bellamy and Dwight, of Griffin and Nettleton, of Alexander and Hodge, my conviction is strengthened that the ministry which is richest in the fruits of holiness is richest in the inculcation of Christian doctrine. I do not see how any man can preach practically who does not preach doctrinally, for the obvious reason that Christian doctrine is truth in theory, and Christian practice is truth in action.

The period of the world which is just opening upon us, is the transition age from a servile submission to ecclesiastical despotism, and the traditions of men to the rights and responsibilities of private judgment; from dominant wickedness to dominant piety; from indifference and inaction to spiritual life and activity; from greedy selfishness to open-handed bounty; from popular ignorance to the wide dissemination of God's word; from the gospel at home to the gospel among all nations; from gross darkness to millennial light and glory. And we feel most deeply that the grand prerequisite to such an age is a more thorough imbuing of the Christian mind with the great truths of the Bible, and an honest, earnest, and abounding deliverance of those truths in distinction from all error, and an intelligent reception of them on the part of the people. If this is no easy matter in a city where the toil and perplexities and responsibilities of business are so urgent and unrelieved, on this very account there is the more reason that Christians, and especially those who bear office in the house of God, should cultivate that enlarged, clear, and discriminating acquaintance with doctrines that shall not only enable them to distinguish between the precious and the vile, but constrain them to require from their religious teachers a full and elaborate exhibition of the rich and varied truths of the glorious gospel of the blessed God.

Of the great object of my ministry, and the manner in which it has been pursued, it becomes me to speak with more than shrinking diffidence. Its revealed object and method are to save the souls of men,—to make them Christians, and the adornment of Christianity. To what extent I have kept this great object in view will be decided by him who will, ere long, judge every man according to his work. Whether I have been devoted to winning souls to Christ, or to other and meaner ends; whether I have declared the whole counsel of God, or have occupied my thoughts and yours on questions to no profit; whether I have sought the praise of men rather than the honor which cometh from God only, and have been stimulated by secular and worldly considerations more than by the love of Christ and of the flock he has committed to my trust; whether I have been influenced by the all-absorbing desire to extend, and build up, and beautify that kingdom of righteousness and peace which shall never have an end, and whether or not, in being thus employed, I have put forth unhallowed hands to the Ark of God, are solemn questions—questions which neither you nor I may trifle with, and which will be decided on that day when appearances will not pass for reality, and nothing will stand the test but truth. I confess these are inquiries which, in this review of my ministry, I am led to look at with mingled solicitude and hope. You have doubtless seen that in me and in my public ministrations which has obscured the light and glory of the gospel I have preached. I implore God's forgiveness for it all, and beg him that it may not be laid to your charge. I am deeply sensible that in my public services there has been the want of a Christlike spirit and tenderness; and that, not unfrequently, in my daily intercourse with you, when I should have been a living epistle, known and read of all men, and should have carried "the bundle of myrrh" in my bosom, I have savored, not the things that be of God, but the things that be of men. Oh! hateful sins, that thus mar the sacred ministry, and cast their shadow over the reminiscences of such a day as this! I have but one refuge:

> "In my hand no price I bring,
> Simply to thy Cross I cling."

My obligations to the God of providence and grace are in every view boundless. He cared for me in my childhood, and kindly gave me the watchful supervision of Christian parents and a Christian training. He cared for me in my youth, and not only restrained me from the excesses of youthful folly and passion, but gave me the opportunity, and directed my mind to the attainment of useful knowledge. He raised me up friends when I most needed them; he encouraged me in my despondency; and when I wandered from him, brought me into his fold. And he put me **into the ministry,** and made me the pastor of this beloved flock. **When I** came among you, I thought it doubtful if I should remain a single year; but he has kept **me** here fifty years. In the midday of human life and in old age he has cared for me, and kept my feet from falling and my soul from death. He has allowed me to pursue my delightful work with no inconsiderable success. He has given me seals to my ministry, which, if my motives have been right, will be my crown of rejoicing in the day of the Lord Jesus. He has **given me** the love and confidence of a united people, and with these tokens of his favor, has also given me "all things richly to enjoy." From year to year he has been mindful of me, though I have so often been unmindful of him. I have said that he has given me all things richly to enjoy; and I am happy to say that he has made you his almoners. Your hearts, your hands, have been the dispensers of his bounty—the more valued that such have been the loved channels through which it has flowed. These tokens of your kindness have made an impression on my mind which it will be difficult to erase. There are trials in the ministry; but it has also its endearments. Scenes and memories like these reflect their rays backward, and diffuse them around us, and throw them onward to cheer those pensive scenes that must soon surround us all. I am looking for them as near at hand; and while I desire to make good use of my last days among you, I know they must be few. I bless God that I do not feel bound to the world as my home, but am more and more sensible that I am a pilgrim and a stranger on the earth. Would that my aspirings after another and better habitation were invigorated in the same proportion as the delusions of earth vanish! I would not build my tabernacle here; it is not among the promises and expectations of time that I look for my resting-place.

Notwithstanding the reminiscences contained in the discourse delivered at the closing service in the old church, we may not suppress all notice of the endeared edifice where the greater part of these fifty years has been employed. We shall not forget **that** time-honored temple of our God and our fathers' **God.** We will carry the remembrance through the remnant of our pilgrimage; it shall **be** inmingled with our sweetest thoughts and hopes, when things earthly are forgotten and the unearthly are remembered; and though they flow from "joys that are past," they shall not be "mournful to the soul." We will carry this remembrance to our dying pillow, and it shall strengthen us upon the bed of languishing. We will carry it beyond the grave, and we will dwell upon it at the **bar** of judgment. **W**e love to look back upon these scenes. There were drops **there** upon the pastures of the wilderness; sometimes falling **drop by** drop, sometimes condensed in clouds, and sometimes rolling **on like the river** which makes glad the city **of** our God. We cannot help looking back upon them with something like the enthusiasm with which the aged warrior surveys the field of battles fought and victories won,—chastened, indeed, elevated, hallowed by the thought that they were victories won in the cause of truth and righteousness, and by a mightier than **human arm.** Beloved sanctuary! **There we were** wont to carry our temporal as well **as our spiritual** troubles, and there were we led to the **Rock** that is higher than we. Oh! how often, as the wing of the pestilence overshadowed us, and the sun smote us by day and the moon by night, have we found there the shadow of the great Rock in a weary land. Blessed, thrice blessed sanctuary, where He that walketh amid the golden candlesticks, and holds the stars in his right hand, made the place of his feet glorious! And that memorable study— so embowered, so retired and tranquil amid noise and uproar, where a desponding heart was so often relieved by the promise, "My grace is sufficient for thee;" where the old and the young so often resorted for consultation and prayer; where volume after volume of God's truth was thrown out upon the world; where the memorials of the divine faithfulness outnumbered even the memorials of man's infirmity; where so many wiped away their tears and began their everlasting song: —Oh! it was the house of God and the gate of heaven! I had thought we had left it forever; but we revisit it to-day: the past instructs us; we retrace the footsteps of him who dwells with man on the earth; we listen to the declaration coming back to us from those ruined walls, "In *all* places where I record my name, I will come unto thee, I will bless thee." Our locality is changed, but the promise remains. God grant that our character as a church may not change, except to growing grace and knowledge and usefulness! We have gained much by the change of locality; it was a struggle to effect it, and has been one of the important objects secured by this ministry. In prospect I regarded it as the last great effort of my life; yet strange to say, at the advanced age of threescore and fifteen years I find that my work is not done. I welcome it still, and as gladly as in the days of my youth. It is God's favor to one sufficiently ill-deserving, to be permitted to bear an equal part in these pulpit ministrations with my more vigorous associate, and to see this beautiful edifice not only completed, but filled to overflowing. Of all the ministers of the gospel in this land, none has greater reason for thankfulness to the God of the sanctuary than he who now addresses you. **I can** scarcely bring myself to believe that the **present** discourse is the *fiftieth* anniversary service **I have** been permitted to enjoy among this people. **These** fifty anniversary discourses—what a history of God's dealings with the Brick church and its pastor, fraught with some reflections that are painful, but with more that are joyous, and in their varied character calling for mingled emotions of sadness and praise!

It is with such emotions, my beloved friends, that I address you to-day. The nearer I approach the time of my departure, the more deeply do I feel interested for your welfare; the more do **I love** you, and long for you all in the bowels of Jesus Christ. **I can** truly say with **the apostle** John, "I have no greater joy than to know that my children *walk in the truth.*" Oh! may the seed that has been planted here, be diligently and faithfully watered by him who is associated with me in the pastoral office. My earnest prayer for this dear flock has been, that God would give them a pastor after his own heart, who should feed them with knowledge and understanding. It would be no small grief to me to go to my grave, and leave this people without a laborious, instructive, faithful ministry. Our hearts, our studies, our consultations ought often to mingle together, that the souls committed to our trust may be saved. The great difficulty ministers find in preaching the gospel is, to lose sight of self. When we can lose sight of ourselves, and be absorbed in the truths we utter; when we can rise above this wicked love of praise, and our minds are wrought up to *speak for God*, we always find that we then have communion with him; and when we have communion with him in our discourses as well as in our prayers, we never fail to come near the consciences and hearts of the people. How sweet such Sabbaths! O for more of the Saviour's compassion and love to the perishing! The Great Shepherd marks every step that we take, hears every prayer we offer, and every sermon we preach. We have but to walk with God, and he shall supply all our need according to the riches of his glory in Christ Jesus.

I will utter but a single thought more. Not a few who hear me, these hands and these lips have baptized into the Christian faith. You were my catechumens, learners of promise, and once bade fair for the kingdom of God. I see you now heads of families. I have performed the same sweet office toward the children God has **given you.** Yet I see you negligent and thoughtless, restraining prayer before God, turning your back upon the cross of Christ, and more than ever lightly esteeming the Rock of your salvation. I know not what more to say to you that I have not already said. This voice you will listen to **but** a little while. **It** is with pain that **I** utter **one** hard thought **in this discourse.** Yet **I** may not suppress the **sentence that if this ministry of fifty years may prove a savor of death unto death, rude will the settlement be of wrath against the** day **of wrath. Will you not seize these** passing hours? **You will soon be crushed** before **the** moth, and in **the** day of your visitation you will need unearthly consolations, and the bosom of a heavenly Parent to lean upon. **And if** you have not this refuge, poor worm of the dust! your house will be left unto you desolate, and the things that belong **to your peace** be hidden from your eyes. **I** shall **soon meet you** at that awful bar, **where these** fifty years **will be remembered.** Will **you not** go from this house **believers in** Jesus, **and live** and die **in** peace? This is the **only ark** of safety for a dying world. How sweet **to be in it** when the windows of heaven are opened, and the deluge is coming down! and there, safe from that desolating storm, and in their contrasted chords and combined harmonies, sing **"the song** of Moses and the song of the Lamb!"

PROCEEDINGS

AT THE

MEMORIAL MEETING.

PROCEEDINGS

AT THE

MEMORIAL MEETING.

The congregation of the Brick Church made arrangements, in August last, to present a memorial to their venerated pastor on the occasion of the fiftieth anniversary of his settlement over them.

On account of the illness of Mrs. Spring at that time, the meeting was postponed to the 15th October, 1860.

At this time the congregation assembled for that purpose in their place of worship. At an early hour the spacious edifice was filled to its utmost capacity.

The meeting was called to order by Shepherd Knapp, Esq., who opened the meeting with the following remarks:—

We have assembled, my respected friends, first of all, as I trust, to render to Almighty God thanks for having permitted so many of us to meet this evening to witness the scene we have here before us; and secondly, to pay a tribute of respect to our beloved pastor, who has, for more than half a century, broken to us so satisfactorily the bread of life. And now, in order, that our proceedings may assume the proper form, I move that HORACE HOLDEN, Esq., be requested to take the chair.

The resolution was adopted.

On motion of Mr. Knapp, Augustus Whitlock and George De Forest Lord, Esqrs., were appointed Secretaries.

The CHAIRMAN on taking the chair spoke as follows:—I thank, you my friends, for calling me to preside upon this occasion. I esteem it one of the sweetest privileges of my life to be permitted, in the good providence of God, to see this night. We have met as a great, affectionate, and united family, to express to our beloved pastor, on this, the fiftieth anniversary of his settlement over us, our undiminished confidence and affection.

As has been properly remarked by my Brother Knapp, in introducing these exercises, devout gratitude and thanks should be first given to Almighty God for the continuance of his care and providence toward this people, and especially for having preserved to us the uninterrupted services of our beloved pastor from the commencement of his ministry to the present hour.

The Rev. Dr. Phillips, pastor of the First Presbyterian church, being then called upon by the Chairman for that purpose, offered prayer and thanksgiving to Almighty God, appropriate to the interesting occasion.

After the prayer, Mr. Holden continued his address as follows:—

Before proceeding to the principal duties of this evening, and the service to be performed by my brother Lord, I may be indulged in a few words to you, my revered pastor—the friend of my youth—of my middle life—and of my grey hairs.

It is not at all probable that one of this vast assembly will ever witness another such occasion as this. Some of us, who have enjoyed the advantages of your ministry for half a century, from the fulness of our hearts may be allowed to speak with perfect freedom.

In this country, of such vast extent, wonderful resources, and enterprise, *the profession of the law* from the very beginning of our national existence has always been considered the surest passport to fortune and to fame!

To this profession, alike honorable and useful, you had been destined in early life. For it you had been educated, and upon its arduous duties you had entered, with every prospect of usefulness and success. All its honors and emoluments were spread out before you. The future was bright and tempting. Industry and learning, intellectual powers, and an unblemished moral character, were capital enough, with which you began your professional career.

It was at an age of our country and of the world, when there was every thing in prospect, to gratify an honorable ambition, founded upon virtuous principle.

But, sir, we desire, here in these courts, thankfully to express our gratitude to God, that at this interesting crisis in your history, you counted none of these things dear unto you, in comparison of the call of God, to preach the unsearchable riches of Christ.

I have been consulting the Records of this church, and I find, that at this juncture, the Brick church became disassociated from the First church.

The venerable Dr. Rodgers, then the sole pastor of this church, greatly beloved for a long life of devotion in his master's service, and bowed down by the infirmities of age, was incapable of discharging the duties of the pastoral office; and the congregation after various ineffectual attempts to agree upon the settlement of a minister, invited you to spend a Sabbath, and preach for them. This invitation was accepted, and on the 4th of June, 1810, resulted in a unanimous call to you to become their pastor; you gave an affirmative answer in the following words :—

ANDOVER, July 6th, 1810.

"*To the Congregation of the Brick Presbyterian Church in the City of New York.*

DEAR BRETHREN:—Your communication, containing a call to me to settle among you, as a gospel minister, has been the subject of advice, prayer and serious deliberation: I hereby accept it: Believe me, dear brethren, that I feel thankful for the unmerited attention and respect, which a call from so respectable a congregation has manifested.

By the blessing of God, I hope to be with you, in the course of a few weeks.

I have given myself to *God:* without recalling that act, I now give myself to *you.* Pray for me fathers and brethren that I may be sent in the fulness of the blessings of the gospel of peace.

Wishing you grace, mercy and peace from God our Father and the Lord Jesus Christ. I am—dear brethren, Your servant in the Lord

GARDINER SPRING.

Deriving no aid whatever, except the paternal advice and counsel of your aged and venerable associate, which you gratefully received and appreciated, the responsibilities of a large congregation were cast entirely upon you.

The next year, the respected and venerable Rodgers was gathered to his father's; and thenceforward you were to stand alone—and you girded yourself for the combat. Of all the venerable men (including *Miller*, *Romeyn*, *Milledoler* and *Perine*) who assisted in your ordination and installation, not one remains.

Here and there, is a solitary individual who stood by your side, when your brown locks, shaded the brow of your youthful prime, and who beheld your rising strength, and who have unceasingly rejoiced in your increasing usefulness.

Amid all the changes we have witnessed in church and state,—all the conflicts of opinion, and strife of parties, we have had reason to rejoice in your firm and unwavering consistency—and, now, that time has gently laid its hand upon you, and your silvered locks bespeak the length of your faithful services, We praise the God of Heaven, and give joyful thanks, that you are still, able, in the maturity of your intellectual vigor, and without interruption to preach the same glorious gospel, in all its simplicity and purity—in all its richness and power.

At the commencement of your ministry among us, the City contained about one hundred thousand inhabitants. Its numbers now approach nearly to a million. During this period, you have seen several generations pass off the stage.

In the venerable old edifice, where for so long a time we were accustomed to worship, you were allowed for forty-six years to hold forth, the words of eternal life to multitudes now scattered throughout this city, and all over this broad land. They still **live** to record with thankfulness their obliga**tions,** and in spirit are with us here to-day—and far greater multitudes, having received the truth in love, have departed in the faith and hopes of the gospel.

In view of our intimate, profitable and happy relations, "which time has made venerable, friendship sweet, and religion sacred," this people gratefully embrace the opportunity, which this fiftieth anniversary affords, of testifying to you their affectionate attachment.

I hope that I shall be excused, if on this **occa**sion, I take the liberty of stating, the **providential** circumstances that first led my youthful footsteps **to** the old Brick church, because I shall describe the experience of many **others.**

In 1809, just one year preceding your settlement, I came, an inexperienced youth to this city to study my profession. Although originally a Presbyterian by education, I had been for a season in the habit of worshipping in an Episcopal church; so that on my arrival here, with prayerbook in hand, **I was** attracted by the earnest zeal **of** the **Rev.** Dr., afterwards Bishop Hobart. Every Sabbath found me regularly in the gallery **of old Trinity.**

It so happened, that I was seldom fortunate enough to hear my favorite preacher; I had not learned the routine of their collegiate mutations, so that I was frequently a hearer of some one, not so captivating to my youthful fancy.

The Rev. Dr. Romeyn had then been settled in Cedar street about one year. I was induced to go and hear him, and soon became a regular attendant in the gallery of his church.

In 1810, Dr. Mason on resigning his pastoral charge in Cedar Street (between Nassau Street and Broadway) occupied Dr. Romeyn's pulpit at half-past twelve o'clock at noon, and in the evening.

Here it was my happiness first to hear, that justly celebrated preacher. I followed him to his new church in Murray street, and was one of his constant hearers and admirers.

Just then New England was convulsed with the uprising of Unitarianism—and you may well suppose, that the anathemas of Dr. Mason, were not tame or infrequent against that monstrous heresy; and there are some who will never forget his severe denunciations also, of New England divinity, and his unmistakable allusions to a certain rising preacher, who was suspected of favoring some peculiar views of the New England school. So captivated was I by the matchless eloquence of Dr. Mason, that, without at first being conscious of the fact, I contracted so strong a prejudice against you, whose face I had never seen, that I could not bear even to hear the sound of the old Brick Church bell.

Inexperienced youth as I was, I shall be pardoned —for I repented.

In justice to Dr. Mason, it becomes me to say, that afterwards he became better acquainted with the young New England divine, and I had the pleasure of seeing him an interested listener to your preaching in the old Brick Church.

In 1814, *Stephen Dodge*, a member of this church, (I mention his name because his Christian fidelity deserves to be recorded,) met me in the street, and invited me **to** accompany him to your *Thursday evening Lecture.* I had never attended an evening religious lecture: I could not resist his polite entreaty. He called for me. He took me **to the** old White Lecture-room, and seated me near the pulpit **among** the elders. The place was **full. It was** a **new** scene to me. I well remember the very spot I occupied on that memorable evening; and well do I remember the text, "If thou, Lord, shouldest mark iniquities, O Lord, who shall stand?" At the end of the meeting all my prejudices had vanished, —and from that night forward I became a regular attendant upon your ministry. *That lecture decided all my future.* It becomes me, with unfeigned humility and deep shame, to confess what a miserable improvement I have made of the inestimable privilege of listening to the gospel from your lips for forty-six years; and yet I must, before all these witnesses, gratefully acknowledge that for all I know of religious truth, I am indebted, under God, to you.

It is no difficult matter to discover the secret of the success which has attended your ministry. We would not "offend your Christian humility," nor indulge in a boastful spirit, in reviewing the past; but gratitude to God requires us to acknowledge the means which he has blessed in making your ministry eminently successful. Your *mind*, in all its powers and faculties, moral and intellectual, has been cultivated with the greatest assiduity, and you have habitually shown that you had a high and grand, as well as *single* aim, in preaching the gospel.

Your *studies* have not only been thorough, systematic, and profound, but various and extensive. Thus qualified, your object has been, not only to enlighten the understanding, but to reach the hearts and consciences of men,—that our fallen nature might be redeemed, purified, and ennobled, and immortal souls fitted for heaven.

In your *preaching* you have always exalted God, and abased the sinner. You have not failed to show men their dependence and their personal ill-desert. And how faithfully have you opened to them clear views of the way of Redemption through Jesus Christ! This has been done, with unwonted tenderness, fidelity, and affection, under a deep impression of divine truth, and with a fervent desire to win souls to Christ.

It has often been matter of amazement to others, how a young man with so short a preparation (even with your intellectual furniture) could have taken **the** entire charge of so large a congregation, and maintained your position among the eminent preachers who adorned the pulpit of 1810.

To a few who remain, who knew the *habits* of your early and later years, and who have watched your course, the secret of your success is readily told. With your untiring industry, you have always borne in mind, and humbly and gratefully acknowledged, your entire dependence upon the gracious influences of the Holy Spirit.

Your *conduct and life* **have always shown what** a high estimate you placed upon the services of the sanctuary; and upon carefully **prepared** written discourses for the *Sabbath*. If the exercises of the pulpit were not sustained habitually and respectably, it was easy to see, that in your view nothing could supply the defect.

God has appointed the *Pulpit* as the chief instrumentality for the salvation of men, and we have been taught by you, from our youth up, that it deservedly holds the preëminence over every other department of ministerial labor.

Your whole life has exemplified this truth. **Y**ou have not been satisfied with flashy discourses. You have taught us that *that* preaching is best which displays the most of God. You have magnified your office in making everything subserve the pulpit, and have shown to us the wide difference between the eloquence of words and the eloquence of thought.

In order that the pulpit should exert its **appropriate influence,** I can triumphantly inquire, Have **you** not striven to feel an interest in every subject presented to your people? Have you not always aimed to be full of your theme? How have you thoroughly studied it! How have you prayed over it! How deeply has the subject of every sermon penetrated your own heart, and like the electric spark, how has it kindled the flame of devotion in the hearts of your hearers; you have not affected a warmth you did not feel; and I must not omit to add, How have all the services of the pulpit been distinguished for their elegant completeness, simplicity, and spirituality! **and how** have the **baptismal font and the** communion table been marked **by the most delicate and** refined dignity and propriety!

Pastoral visitation has always received an appropriate **share of** your attention. This you have taught us to esteem a valuable means of grace; but if pastoral visitation or the pulpit must be neglected the former must give way.

There have been times, many memorable seasons **in your** history, when God, in his infinite mercy, **has been** pleased to grant to this people the **out-**

pouring of the Holy Spirit. *Then* what a delightful duty it was, and how cheerfully did you improve the privilege, of going from family to family to guide inquiring souls, cheer the faint, comfort the feeble-minded, to satiate the weary, and replenish the sorrowful soul!

In these delightful seasons, not one weary, heavy-laden sinner was ever overlooked. There always have been, and always will be, very pressing, if not unreasonable demands upon a minister's time for pastoral visitation. It would be marvellous indeed, if there were not isolated instances in which there were not at least apparent omissions of this **duty** on your part. In all my long intercourse with you and with the people whom you have so faithfully served, **I do** not recollect to have heard of an instance **in** which a pastoral visit was neglected, if there was any real call for it, or the least prospect of doing any good.

Who was ever sick and languishing—smitten of God and afflicted—that did not receive your most prompt attention! If sickness and death could speak, what revelations would be made of sweetest sympathy—of the kindest and most faithful instructions! What words of consolation and hope to **the** afflicted and sorrowful believer! How do the sounds of tender, sweet, soul-subduing prayer still linger on the ear! And when death has come up into our windows, the sound of whose footsteps first broke upon our sad silence! Whose voice of heavenly consolation first soothed our bleeding hearts!

In a word, you have always appropriated your time in such a way, in public and in private, that it should accomplish most for the honor of God, and the good of your fellow-men. *Time*, with which so many trifle, and of which almost all men are prodigal, has been diligently employed by you in the service of this people.

To gratify the popular ear and taste has never been the object of your ministry. Your preaching has not been a mere playing with the imagination and passions at a distance from divine truth. Nor have you ever indulged in a style which pleased the fancy of worldly men without reaching their conscience. Your theology has afforded the best field for tender, solemn, and sublime eloquence. "**The system** of theology," prepared with great **labor by you, not for the** schools but for the people, **will never** be forgotten by those who were so highly favored **as to** hear it.

In 1816 **and** onward, I was acquainted with a number of young men, of well-informed minds and cultivated taste, who were in the habit of listening to those doctrinal discourses, (among the most important and effective, in my humble judgment, you ever preached;) and when the sermon was the theme **of** discussion afterwards, while some approved—

none actually reviled—others bitterly complained that they were "hard sayings, who could hear them." Mark the sequel: these very complaining young men were the first, on each successive Sabbath, to occupy their wonted places in the sanctuary, and to listen with increasing interest to these searching, humbling, weighty truths. Many of these young men, if not all, became signal trophies of redeeming grace. In this way you did much to elevate the tone of Biblical knowledge and piety. Multitudes with a new interest began to search the scriptures, and through your instrumentality a large number of them devoted themselves to the ministry.

In exhibiting the distinguishing doctrines of **the** gospel, without courting opposition or making yourself needlessly offensive, you have not shunned to resist fanaticism and spurious religious excitements. You have aimed to preach the whole truth in simplicity and godly sincerity.

During all these fifty years you have rebuked our pride and reproved our worldliness; you have set our sins before us, you have warned us of the coming wrath, and you have exhibited to us the cross in all its sublime and holy attractions. **In** what persuasive accents have you commended to our acceptance the infinitely compassionate Saviour! and how have you urged us, by all the allurements of his love, to the everlasting enjoyment of his rest!

You have baptized our children, and our children's children, for several generations; and great numbers of them you have helped us to deposit in the grave, in the sweet hope of that glorious morning, when they that sleep in Jesus shall awake in his likeness.

I need not allude to the many printed volumes which you have sent forth, to instruct and edify your fellow-men. They speak for themselves. They will prove an enduring monument of your intellectual vigor, and of your consistent, mature, and warm-hearted piety.

While an enlightened and liberal charity has ever kept you within the bounds of kindness toward those who differed from you in opinion, you have not been induced to depart from the high standard of evangelical truth which has ever distinguished your ministry.

In all *seasons of calamity*, during plague and pestilence, personal peril and public danger, you have always been at your post, and, with unflinching fidelity and devotion, ministered to the wants of the sick and the dying, and comforted the sorrowful and the bereaved.

During the many gracious visitations with which this church has been blessed under your labors, it were no easy task truthfully to describe the deep and sweet solemnity which has pervaded our assemblies.

"How sweet and how awful was the place!" What days of heaven upon earth! no tongue can describe them. How lovely the sanctuary! every **pew filled, the** galleries crowded in every part with anxious and devout worshippers. What tokens of the divine **presence!** what pledges of his love! What a beautiful and sublime spectacle, to behold the vast assembly, retiring after each service, *in profound silence, to meditate and pray.*

Amid these scenes of mercy, it is delightful to know that almost every member of the church was actively employed.

In addition to the services of the sanctuary, the weekly lecture, and the ordinary prayer-meetings, there were maintained for a long period twelve **neighborhood** prayer-meetings, at private houses, on every Friday evening, in different **parts** of the congregation, sustained by committees averaging seven each, which were so distributed as every week to ensure a continual rotation. All these efforts received your watchful supervision.

The *Old White Lecture-room*, so redolent with the richest perfume during these halcyon days, claims here a **passing** tribute. What a fountain of sweet memories does its simple name unseal! Here was the scene of some of your most successful labors. What deep and pungent convictions **of sin!** What penitential sighings! What tears **of** contrition! What heart throbbings! **What** numerous conversions! What songs of triumphant rejoicing! It must be reserved for eternity to recount the triumphs of grace witnessed in the Old White Lecture-room.

In these memorable days, the manifestation of the divine presence was often so evident, that we seemed every time we entered the sanctuary to hear God's declaration to Moses, as if audibly repeated: "Put off thy shoes from off thy feet, for the place whereon thou standest is holy ground." Then did the great Master of Assemblies walk amid the golden candlesticks, and make the place of his feet glorious.

These were days and scenes never to be forgotten. It is refreshing to look back upon them, and give God thanks for these bright spots in your history.

That great and gracious Being, "in whose hand our breath is, and whose are all our ways," has been pleased to spare you, while you have seen all your compeers laid in the grave. It is pleasant, yet mournful at this hour, to recall the names of some of the officers of this church, who labored most harmoniously with you, and who have gone to their rest on high.

I may not omit to mention the sedate and venerable *Bingham;* the warm-hearted and heavenly-minded *Whitlock;* the meek and childlike *Cunningham;* the intelligent and upright *Hawes;* the wise and useful *Lockwood*; the respected and pious *Havens*; the courteous *Bulkley*; the conservative and gentlemanly *De Forest*; the sober-minded *Stephens*; the urbane and gentle *Halsey*; the amiable and exemplary *Oakley*; the earnest and devout *Bokee*; the humble, lowly, and refined *McComb*; the guileless and unassuming *Brown*; the modest and diffident *Luyster*; the sincere and unpretending *Mead*; the consistent and devoted *Harding*; and *Adams*, the inflexible and just. Their record is on high.

It would be most gratifying, if time permitted, to review the rise and progress of the *various benevolent and religious enterprises* which have arisen during **your** ministry, and in which you have borne a conspicuous part. They **are** the glory of our **land**. The triumphs of the gospel, in this and in other lands, have distinguished this period beyond **all** others. Science and the arts, education and literature, have made advances such as the world never before saw.

During all this time, what could have been accomplished without the *pulpit?* And may I not appeal to this great assembly, and confidently ask, "How important and appropriate a share has this **pulpit** borne in the glorious work of saving the world?"

The part you have been permitted to bear in **these** heaven-born enterprises, and in demonstrating the power of the pulpit as the most important agency in converting the world, will be remembered with sincerest gratitude by all coming generations.

The joyful solemnities of this interesting hour, **which** must be limited in continuance, will not **allow of** even a rapid glance at numerous other topics which crowd upon our memories.

I cannot, I dare not, however, in justice to my**self, and** to "all these **children** whom God hath given you," omit to say, that we **are** indebted to your ministry more than to anything and all things else beside, on earth. "*The things that are seen are temporal.*" We can only say, out of our full hearts, We love you sincerely, ardently love you, and here in these courts record it.

I should be derelict in duty, and do violence to the best feelings of my nature, if I should neglect on this occasion to pay my feeble tribute of grateful respect and love to the memory of that **beloved** Woman, who for upwards of fifty-four **years** was the companion of your toils and the **sharer** of your joys.

From the very beginning of your ministry, with a clear and sagacious intellect, and "a zeal according to knowledge," she identified herself with all your interests and **duties as pastor of** this people: to a clear and discriminating mind, she united excellent judgment and piety.

Her social qualities were of a high order, and,

combined with her courteous demeanor, secured the confidence and esteem of the whole congregation.

Those **of** this congregation who have known the **large** family which she reared, will require no enumeration from me of her peculiar traits, to magnify the amount of care, of toil, of night-watchings; or the patience, economy, prudence, and solicitude which she uniformly exhibited during your whole ministry.

"She worked willingly with her hands. She looked well to the ways of her household. She never ate the bread of idleness. Strength and honor were her clothing."

Comparatively very few of this **people** have **ever** known how **much** they were indebted to her **watch**-fulness and industry. When **oppressed and** overburdened with the responsibilities and cares of a large congregation, how, with a device and forethought which faithful woman only knows, did she interpose her willing hand and heart to relieve you of domestic toil, and prudently, studiously, and industriously superintend all your household affairs, with a vigilance that never slept!

It would be difficult to describe the labors, the anxieties, the perplexities of which she relieved you, when she knew that the claims of your people and your preparations for the pulpit made constant demands upon **your** time and vigor equal to your utmost capacity.

Her encouraging look, her prudent endearments and cheerful smile, amid all her cares and duties, have often chased away your despondency, and bade you go on your way rejoicing.

God, in his infinite wisdom, has seen fit to take her to himself. "She has gone to a scene where her virtues will not miss their employment." "Her children arise up, and call her blessed. Her husband also, and he praiseth her."

But I must close.

Long, my revered pastor, may you stand in this pulpit. May the rich lessons of experience and love from your exhaustless storehouse, (garnered there by fifty years of untiring industry,) continue to flow from your lips, to edify and comfort an affectionate and devoted people, for a great while to come.

May he, who hath hitherto so kindly watched over you, deal gently with you now in this hour of your trial. May he fill you with his Spirit, comfort you with his presence, and ever enlighten your path, until the evening sun of a long and well-spent day shall shine serenely upon the closing scene, and the blessed Saviour, taking you by the hand, lead you peacefully and triumphantly through the dark valley.

"His rod and his staff comfort you."

DANIEL LORD'S ADDRESS.

The chairman having announced the order of the exercises, DANIEL LORD, Esq., delivered the following address. He said:

Fifty years ministering to the same people! What a remarkable event in the history of a congregation! remarkable in the long service of the minister, and in the steady love and satisfaction of his people. It calls for the expression of devout thankfulness to God by both. It deserves to be perpetuated by a durable memorial, and warrants a mutual congratulation.

Fifty years of labor in an intellectual, arduous, and painful vocation! Fifty years of such toil permitted to be exercised by one pastor, and to be enjoyed by one community! It involves a vast thought! The venerated dead who have been named to you as once here,—where are they? Fifty years upon them! They have passed away; but they are witnesses still with us. For here we have been taught, that the end of this gospel is to bring those who are faithful to the spirits of just men made perfect. It adds to the sacredness of this occasion and of this place, that we believe that the spirits of the "just made perfect" look down with favor at all that is worthy in these celebrations.

Fifty years of pastoral service! What a mass of labor! Two orations a week, one or two studied discourses, and innumerable calls for intelligent instruction, and sacred and holy counsels! Fifty years' service! Why, what effect ought it to produce! My friend has spoken of those who were aged. But how many have come up from childhood, and grown old during those fifty years! I remember the gentlemen who have been named, when I was a boy, a child: they are gone, but are they the only ones who have partaken in the services which we now commemorate? Generations have risen up, grown old, and passed away, under this ministration of fifty years. Fifty years spared to an intellectual man! Thanks are due to God for so great a mercy. Not fifty dragging years, which merely leave upon the calendar the marks of so many items of duration, but fifty years of labor, fifty years of motion, fifty years of eloquence, fifty years culminating, not in debility, but in vigor; not in the leanness of old age, but in the fatness of intellectual strength! Thanks be to God for so great a mercy!

This occasion calls on us to look at another thing in this result of fifty years. It has been fifty years of concord in this excited city—fifty years of American life—fifty years of a changing population—fifty years of a congregation united, under circumstances not always the most easy to be harmonious in—

fifty years of real Christian unity in one congregation! It is a circumstance not to be proud of,— for man alone could not do it; but it is a thing to be thankful for, because it does seem to be an evidence of God's presence.

Let us look for a moment at the people among whom these fifty years have been spent, not in the way of self-gratulation, but of a sober estimate of the progress of which we are now speaking. It is a part of the history of this church, that in the Revolution it was the Democratic part of the larger Presbyterian church which comprised it. It was the patriotic, in opposition to the conservative and Tory part of the Presbyterian body in this city. The Scotch and Irish elements were vastly conservative; the American element, the New England element, settled itself in that edifice of which **we**, as the successors, are worshippers. Our predecessors were of those who, in the Presbyterian community as in every other, form the middle class, and are at once the basis and the bond of society. As time rolled on, these men, according to the natural thrift of an industrious people, became a powerful community; and in 1809, after this Revolutionary toil had all passed over, and its memory had become in some degree forgotten, there was **a** necessary division in the larger body of which this congregation was a part. But here remained the descendants of those hard working, hard thinking, independent men. As I remember this community in early life, the Brick Church congregation was composed of men in the middle ranks of life—thinking, working, independent men—men whom you could not drive by fear, nor coax by favor, and with whom you could not deal without intellectual conviction. Convince them, and they were yours; fail to convince them, and they were the most independent body of men that could be seen. Now it was among such a people as that, that this fifty years' ministry began. It was to a people like this, that our esteemed friend was called to minister. This people underwent those changes in our history which, when I mark them to you, will show that there did exist causes of dissension, of difficulty, of controversy, things uncongenial with that harmony which always has existed among us. We had the war of 1812, with all its exciting political questions,—questions which, though they were political, really went into the very bosom of every man's family. We had the most severe party controversies following upon that war. Then came the period of religious enterprise—the establishment of the great charities outside of the church, endeavoring to combine men of all descriptions in the same course of charity. But that infirmity which belongs to all human things led to divisions of opinion, and to excitement respecting them. Then we came upon the times of slavery and antislavery. These questions touched us at every point, and they were questions to which the pastor **was not a** stranger. He had his opinions, and **they** were not concealed nor withheld. But how did he deal with his people, amid these topics of excitement and distraction? He took the philosophic ground, that if the fountain was pure the stream would be clean. He did not go down to stop the mouth of the river, but he sought to clear it at the source. He went upon the gospel principle, that a regenerated heart with an enlightened conscience would follow out every religious principle to **its** true practice. **It** was his office, and charge me **not** with adulation for saying I **think he fulfilled it. Those** who would go too far, and were **in** danger **of** becoming fanatical, found in him the man to discourage them; and those who **were** cold, and would not go far enough, felt the excitements of his preaching. It was not necessary for him to mingle otherwise with the controversies of the day; it was enough for him to furnish the Christian man with the antidote against that which was within him, and the armor against that which was **without.** And it does seem to me that, under no other **mode** of ministration, in the circumstances through which we have passed, could the people **have been kept** so harmonious. Upon those great principles of the gospel all men could unite; and by reason of that spirit of harmony we have passed through struggles and difficulties of the gravest sort. We passed through this period of trial through the difficult, the very difficult, although apparently insignificant, process of settling upon a new place of worship, a subject upon which many congregations have broken. We have harmoniously called to his aid a colleague. All this has taken place in consequence of that spirit of harmony, which has grown **out of** the preaching **of the** simple gospel as the remedy for all the evils marking both the individual and social state.

I have already spoken of the general drift of his ministrations;—the degree and manner in which they have been exercised we ought not to fail to notice. And I do it in no spirit of exaggeration,—in no spirit of wonder. The deeds of a giant, although they might be great in themselves, would be but a poor example to hold up, because but few **can** be giants; and where the actions done are very extraordinary, the benefit of the example is lost. **What** strikes me as particularly calling for our thanks **to** God upon this occasion is, that the results which have been produced, so beautiful to look at, have been such as are within the reach of ordinary men, with ordinary prudence, zeal, and labor; and that, while the endurance of life and vigor has in the present case **been** extraordinary, **in** no other respect has that which has been done here been that which may not be done any where.

But it has been a toilsome and laborious office. I have no belief in genius, except that it is a great capacity for labor. **We** have had labors **in** season and out of season, labors of the mind and labors of the heart, labors burdened with thoughts of the consequences which waited upon them : of these we have had the enjoyment, and of these we now reap the blessings. It was a duty to labor. I am sure that our friend would say, "Laboring as I have, I have not done all that I ought to have done." To us, who look at and have enjoyed them, his labors have been great; we appreciate them, and we cheerfully pay the tribute of our acknowledgment.

Dear Sir, you have labored, and you have labored **well.**

Labored how ? In the ministry of the **gospel** :— **a** labor not of meditation and thinking merely, but **of** learning also—in which was involved not only the production of your own best thoughts, but of the rich thoughts given by holy men to the improvement of the world. That ministry which is not enriched by the learning of the wise and holy is like the pool into which no stream flows, which no spring supplies, and daily grows shallow, muddy, and unrefreshing. We therefore call upon the minister of the word, and do it **rightly, that he** shall not only be thoughtful, but studious and learned, **if we are to** anoint him faithful.

Such a man we have had. The duties of such a

life have been absorbing. Its requirements shut out a routine of polite, or of merely civil and unnecessary participation in all the smaller concerns of the congregation. Those who, in this or any other considerate congregation, should have expected this, ought to have been, and must have been, disappointed. Such a course would be inconsistent with the dignity of a learned, laborious, and painstaking minister. Such has been the ministry we acknowledge; yet, when reverses, when affliction, when distress came, in any shape, we never lacked his counsel and tenderest sympathy; especially—and I turn to it with great emphasis—we never lacked fitting prayer. I cannot pass by the fact of the particular appropriateness of the services which we have enjoyed in the matter of occasional prayer. Let this congregation turn their memories to any event in which there was a peculiarity, an affliction, a calamity, or a remarkable cause of joy, and let me ask, if the supplications by their minister in his services, public or private, were not of the tenderest sympathy, of the wisest and best desires, pointing to the aid from on high which was most clearly needed.

It is but just that this congregation should, by the tribute which we now bring, acknowledge with thanks to God, these laborious services so long enjoyed.

But this memorial has another trait of deep significance. We do what we can to put honor, so far as man may, on the ministry as a lofty calling. It is intellectual in the highest degree. It demands **great** personal devotion, sacrifices, and efforts. It exacts a social and moral purity, for which unaided human nature almost seems incapable. When men in this calling have faithfully earned the approbation of those who have witnessed their achievements, why should they not have their ovations and their triumphs? Soldiers and statesmen have their inferior exploits celebrated by triumphs and triumphal arches, and perpetuated by the decorations of sculpture and of painting. **Why** should not this profession, renouncing to a **great extent, as they** do, **the profitable** emoluments of **intellectual labor and** secular enterprise,—why, I say, **should not they** receive something that shall be like a statue, a picture, or an arch, something which shall be, not to themselves only, but to their posterity and the world, an acknowledgment of excellence and success?

It is in this sense that my heart unites in this tribute, both as a member of this congregation and **as a man.** Looking at large upon the influence of this magnanimous profession upon the great interests of the world, I can only say that it **was well** summed up in the account of his fifty years' ministry by our esteemed friend, **in** the comprehensive thought, Redemption;—the Redemption of the world from sin, from the power **of sin**; the buying out from captivity of the souls of men: Redemption, the effect of which, as he showed us upon another still later occasion, is the bringing of those **who** receive it, to the spirits of just men made perfect. On which occasion, was not the resurrection of the dead brought before us, not as a dogma, but **as a household, personal,** and domestic truth, **telling** us (and it touches my very heart) that those of us who attain the average length of life, if we reach heaven, shall there find more to receive us with joy, than we shall have left here to mourn us? This congregation, therefore, rightly judge and feel that the gift we have to make is justified and deserved by every consideration.

It is a gift of intrinsic value. It may well be that an earthen cup and pitcher would serve the material wants as well as the costly testimonial which we desire to lay before our Pastor. But **that** beautiful incident strikes me forcibly, wherein **a woman took a box of** very costly ointment, and poured it out in what seemed to be a waste; and it was asked why it was not sold, and the price given to the poor. A lesson was then taught, that nothing can be a waste, however costly, which consecrates, ornaments, and perpetuates a great Christain sentiment or principle. If it is a principle worth consecrating, worth perpetuating, that the ministry of the gospel is a great and an elevated office, and that it should be faithfully executed, and that it is deserving of honor when so executed, then, valuable as this gift is, nay, were it ten times more **valuable, it** would be but appropriate. With **these** views, and in behalf of those offering this testimonial, I beg leave to read, for the sanction of **this** assembly, this letter of presentation :—

REVEREND AND DEAR SIR :—

The people of your charge unite with you in thanks to God, for having enjoyed with you the fiftieth year of your ministry among them.

They gratefully acknowledge the faithfulness of your services to their fathers and themselves, in preaching **to them** the gospel of Christ, with sincerity and singleness of purpose, with prayer and **labor, not** having **in your view the** fear or favor of man, but the honor and glory **of God, in** advancing the kingdom of his Son; and having before you chiefly the consecration to him of the love and service of those who are committed to your charge.

They cannot (as they ought not) forbear to express to you their thanks and love for your sympathy in their joys and prosperity, and in their afflictions and bereavements; nor can they fail **to** acknowledge you as the tender friend, **as well as** the counsellor to sacred duties and the minister of heavenly consolation.

They, with the Christian multitudes of our country, look upon you as having an honorable place in its sacred literature, whose printed words will continue to advance the object of your ministry after you shall have entered into rest.

They also bear witness to your usefulness as a public-spirited Christian man, in the councils of the church at large, and in the literary, religious, and benevolent institutions of your age, bringing, not only thoughts of wisdom, but words of peace.

As a slight mark of their esteem, they now ask your acceptance of a durable expression and memorial of their friendship and love, and of their sincere and abiding reverence.

Mr. Lord moved the adoption by the meeting of the Address of Presentation.

The motion was seconded by Jasper Corning, Esq., who spoke as follows:—

ADDRESS OF MR. CORNING.

I esteem it a great privilege, sir, to have the opportunity of seconding this interesting memorial which has just been read by Mr. Lord. When I look around upon this large audience, and after the interesting history of this church which has been given by my two predecessors, it seems to be almost presumptuous for me to say anything; but when I cast my mind back for about forty-nine years, to the time when I was first connected with this people, and with this beloved pastor, I must say a word of thankfulness and gratitude to him for the instructions which he gave me in my youth, and for my first vivid and solemn impressions of the truth of God caused by the words that fell from his lips upon that Sabbath when I first entered the old Brick Church in 1811. Never shall I forget it. And when the first communion season came,—but I need not tell you, who have sat under his ministry, of the solemnity which always pervades that interesting season of communion instituted by our Lord and Saviour, when he brake the bread and distributed it, with the cup. And when I heard our pastor's impressive remarks, his persuasive and soul-thrilling arguments, my heart and conscience were pierced. Those feelings never left me, and by the grace of God, I trust they were followed by the renovation of my heart. I thank you, my dear sir, [turning to Dr. Spring,] for all that affectionate instruction which you gave me in the heat of my youth,—in my forwardness and abruptness. I well remember when you placed your hand upon my head, and said, "Not so fast, my son; gently." Never shall I forget it.

Very few of the persons here present know the fact that this beloved pastor, for the first two or three years of his ministry, was a delicate man. He was not little, as I was about to say, for he was tall; but he was so feeble in health that the congregation obtained an assistant for three months at one time to aid him in his labors. What reasons for thankfulness to God have we when we see him here to-night, and when we heard him, a few weeks ago, deliver his fiftieth anniversary sermon in this *second temple*. But when I think of those beloved departed ones to whom I once used to look up with such reverence, respect, and affection, I feel saddened:—Mills, **Whitlock**, Prince, Havens, Adams, Cunningham, and many others—time would fail me to state the whole number,—for there was a period in the history of this church when there were sixty men upon whom that beloved pastor could call to lead in prayer. Where is there such a church now? We have spoken and you have heard of the tribute of respect that is to be paid to him to-night; but what is that compared with the glorious tribute which is all around him to-night?

As I again look around upon your faces, and think of the generations, one by one, whom he has baptized and received into the fellowship of the church, I pray, and you will pray, that he may be spared yet many years, to gather in that other generation of children which is just arising here. Would not that be the crowning glory of his life? to see another outpouring of the Spirit of God here, such as those which he has already seen, and I have seen, and many others, also, have seen, in this congregation,—to gather in one more blessed harvest of the lambs of the flock to present to his Saviour, before going on high to receive his crown of **glory**. Oh! how blessed is the truth, that they who turn many unto righteousness shall shine as stars **in** the firmament for ever and ever! I pray God that he may be spared yet many years for this holy service; and that, when God in his holy providence shall say to him, Come up higher, his mantle may fall upon you, my beloved friend, [Dr. Hoge,] that you may be a happy and successful minister of the gospel; and that you, too, may, if it is God's will, see your fiftieth anniversary.

I second that motion, sir, with **the greatest** pleasure.

The Chairman put **the** question, when the **address** was unanimously adopted. The service of plate was then formally presented.

REV. DR. SPRING'S REPLY.

It does not become me, Mr. Chairman, **to** occupy your time to-night. It is a very humble part which I may bear in these exercises. You have given me fifty years of active service among you; and I am more than satisfied to resign to my friends this passing hour. They will certainly excuse me from preaching to them now; it is their turn to preach to me. And I may well honor their ingenuity in that they have already been able to say so much upon so bald a theme.

I have listened with thankfulness to words of attachment and confidence, and even to words of high commendation. These kind thoughts, so commendatory of my character and course, as well as this beautiful and splendid expression of your bounty, affect me. I am embarrassed by them. They oppress me. They make me ashamed, because they remind me of so many defects in my character, and so many shortcomings in my ministry. Indeed, my beloved flock, I am not worthy of such commendations.

But while they humble me, they make me thankful—thankful to God because he **has** given me a loving and munificent people, and thankful to you that **you** are not ashamed of your pastor. **There** are trials in the Christian ministry, and it also has its endearments. Scenes like these, and such expressions of love and confidence from intelligent minds and sanctified hearts, are fitted to encourage me in my work; and, next to the light of God's countenance, they will light **up** my passage to the grave. I have not anticipated a gloomy old age, though now and then a sombre coloring has flitted across my imagination in view of the future. But whatever have been my apprehensions, you have thrown light upon my path this evening, and I shall leave this sanctuary to-night, feeling that I may yet go on my way among you, and rejoice as I go. Many a time have I offered the prayer, that I might not be allowed to be a cumberer of the ground; and I repeat it now. But while I do so, it is not with a desponding mind; nor will I yield to discouragement so long as I have your testimony that my imperfect services are not only profitable to others, but creditable to myself. There are yet new fields of copious thought before me, which though I despair of overtaking, on the outskirts of which we may perhaps yet travel together and reap **the** ripening harvest.

As to the past fifty years of my ministry among you, I have little to say. "Ye are my glory and joy." My object has been single. It has been to do some good in the world, in the pulpit, and through the press. I have been "*your* servant for Jesus' sake," and the servant of no other set of men. My time, my studies, my influence, my heart, have been yours. I have ever regarded it as a wise maxim, to endeavor to do one thing well, rather than many things indifferently; and therefore have **been** *your minister*. That I have come short of this high mark, I well know. Yet this has been my aim—often, I trust, calling to my remembrance that I am "set to watch for souls as one who must give an account."

But, my fellow-men, much of the credit here to-night belongs to you; and but a very small portion of it belongs to me. I have been surrounded by men for the past fifty years, who have held up my hands by their counsel, by their example, and by their prayers. Many a time, as was alluded to by my friend who introduced those resolutions, we were upon the **very verge of** dissolution, and it seemed to the most thoughtful actually impossible to keep the congregation from being cleaved asunder; but that God, whose hand is upon all things, spiritual and moral, came to our aid, and we remained a united people. As my friend Lord said, they were God's influences, **added** to the moral influences of truth, that have preserved us as we are. It was my privilege to have what in modern literature is called a prestige, which has **been** much **in my** favor. I entered upon the work under the influence of a great name.

My venerable predecessor, the Rev. Dr. John Rodgers, whose last official act was to lay his hands upon my youthful head and lead the Presbytery in the ordination service, on the 8th of August, 1810, may not be forgotten on such a day as this. He was the Father of Presbyterianism in this city, and the founder of the Brick Church. And I will express the hope that ere long a tablet to his memory will be erected in the edifice in which we stand.

There is another tablet too, you have lately erected, in memory of one who entered upon this field of labor with me, and whose cheerful devotement to your interests and mine deserves a place in all our hearts. Pardon me if I ask you to take a few steps to yonder vault, and aid me, in this glad hour, in weaving a laurel wreath around the head of her who for fifty years labored with me as an efficient helper in my responsible labors.

But above all would I give honor to the God of heaven,—and, what has not a little delighted me, my friends who have preceded me have thought of him. Mr. Chairman, let the God of Zion be exalted.

In thankfulness I have listened to those remarks, and I accept this token of your favor with gratitude.

Dr. Spring then offered the following resolution, which was adopted:—

Resolved, That the Session and Board of Trustees of this church be requested to consider the propriety of erecting a suitable tablet to the memory of the late Dr. John Rodgers, in some part of this edifice.

Dr. Rodgers, grandson of Dr. John Rodgers, returned thanks.

The Rev. Dr. Krebs then presented and read an Address from the Presbytery of New York, prefacing it with the following remarks:

ADDRESS OF THE REV. DR. KREBS.

Dr. Spring :—My dear Sir, my honored Friend and Father: I think myself happy in having been selected by your Co-Presbyters and mine to be the organ of their communication with you upon this interesting occasion. But it would ill become me to occupy this time with the expression of my personal feelings. I am charged with the presentation to you of the sentiments of your brethren in the ministry of Jesus Christ. When it was made known to them, about the beginning of July, that the people of this congregation designed this commemorative service, which was at first appointed for the sixth of August, they immediately arranged to be represented in it. And, although the appointment was necessarily postponed by the affecting event which, when we call to mind its circumstances and coincidences, we cannot help regarding as an EUTHANASIA, it has not been thought proper to make any alteration of the Address which had been prepared. I have now the happiness of presenting it to you in the name of the Presbytery

Dr. Krebs then read the Address as follows:

ADDRESS OF THE PRESBYTERY OF NEW YORK.

To the Rev. Gardiner Spring, D.D., LL.D.,

Our Venerable Co-Presbyter and Beloved Bro. in the Gospel Ministry:

The Presbytery of New York, having learned with great satisfaction that it is proposed **by the** congregation of the Brick Presbyterian Church in this city to commemorate, on the **sixth day of August, the** fiftieth anniversary **of** your ordination and instalment as their pastor, unanimously agreed to avail themselves of the occasion to present to you, through the undersigned, their affectionate salutations and recognition of the interesting event.

During this period of your active life, you have been a spectator of the wonderful progress which has marked the history of the world and of our own country, recorded within this interval. You have seen the equally wonderful progress of the church of God, and of **our own church,** widely extended through this land, and spreading with missionary enterprise among **the** heathen. You have seen this great city growing from a few score thousands to nearly a million of inhabitants, and enriched **and** adorned with **wealth**, with institutions of religion, learning, and art, and achieving mighty influence, until it has already become the third among the capitals of Christendom, and **is aspiring to be the commercial** capital of the world. **You have** seen the churches of our Order, from **less than** half a score **in** number, multiplied ten**fold, and** strengthened with many tokens **of** gracious revival and divine blessing; **and** you have borne a favored part therein. You have seen many of them—including the Old Brick **itself,** venerable with sacred and historic associations—removed with the advance of population and prosperity from the sites where they were originally established, to better positions, and more convenient and beautiful edifices.

It has pleased him who appoints the number of our months and determines the bounds of our habitation, to prolong your days with vigor, and **your** ministry with abundant usefulness,—while you have seen all who in this city were your contemporaries in the ministry at the commencement of your own, passing away. The fathers, where are they? and the prophets, do they live for ever? The aged members of this congregation who, then here, solicited and witnessed your ordination, are **all** gone. Even that younger band, who stood around you and welcomed you as their pastor while yet the dew of your youth was upon you, and they too were blossoming with promise, are represented by a few hoary heads. The names of the rest of them have been transferred from the registries of this church to monumental stone. Their enduring record is on high.

Of the members of the Presbytery at the time of your ordination, not one survives among us. Of all who succeeded them, and compose it now, every one admitted with your consent, no small proportion has come into human life within the period of your prolonged pastorate.

We salute you as the Father of the Presbytery. We hail, with you, this day, the completion of half a century spent in the ministry of our adorable Lord and Saviour, and in your first and only pastorate laboriously and happily devoted to the edification of one congregation,—surpassing even the prolonged service of the sainted Rodgers in the same field,—an example, the first in our history as a Presbytery and in this city, and any where as rare as it is beautiful and touching, especially in these times of restlessness and change.

We are glad to acknowledge the dignity, courtesy, and kindness which have impressed upon your younger brethren the wise counsels by which our conferences and deliberations have been assisted,—the encouragement we have derived from your coöperation in works and labors of love,—

the comfort of **your sympathy** in trials,—and **the force of your personal example** and unstained character, **and of all the grace of God that** was with you,—whereby the common salvation **has been promoted, our** intercourse with you **and with each other has been so harmonious and** so happy, **and our love and veneration** for your person and ministry **have been continually** enlarged.

We rejoice with you in the long and beautiful **attachment of the people among whom you have passed your ministry in all** good **prosperity and honor,**—in their recent consideration and care **to** lighten **the labors of** your declining years by giving to you a colleague in your pastoral office,—and in this present demonstration of their continued affection and respect.

Our prayers are joined with them that your days to come may yet **be** long,—like the palm-tree planted in the house of the Lord, and flourishing **in the** courts of our God, and **bringing forth** fruit **in old age.** And when all your work is done, **may your last** look on the world be cheered with **the sight** of the Redeemer's kingdom advancing, and your **peaceful** departure be followed with an abundant entrance **into that glorious kingdom, where** they that be wise shall shine **as** the brightness of **the** firmament, and they **that turn** many to righteousness as the stars for ever and ever.

We subscribe ourselves, your brethren in the

gospel of our Lord, on behalf of the Presbytery of New York,

JOHN M. KREBS,
Pastor of the Rutgers Street Church.

W. W. PHILLIPS,
Pastor of the 1st Pres. Ch. in New York.

R. McCARTEE,
Pastor Westminster Church, New York.

EBENEZER PLATT,
Ruling Elder in Rutgers Street Church.

WM. WALKER,
Ruling Elder Pres. Ch., 5th Av. & 19th St.

NEW YORK, JULY, 1860.

At its conclusion, Dr. Spring replied by **a bow**. He then said **that a** beloved brother, Rev. **Dr.** Samuel Spring, of Hartford, had expected to be present on this occasion, but as he had been detained by sickness, he had kindly sent his address in manuscript. Dr. Spring, therefore, moved that his son, GARDINER SPRING, Jr., Esq., should be requested to read it in behalf of his uncle. The motion was adopted, and Mr. Spring then read the address, as follows:

ADDRESS OF REV. SAMUEL **SPRING**, D. D.

MR. CHAIRMAN:—With no design of throwing a shade of pensiveness over a most joyous proceeding, I yet find it difficult to suppress the thought that there is one element wanting to complete our satisfaction here, where there is so **much** to animate, and so much to awaken gratitude. I look around **upon this** gathering of my brother's flock, and my **brother's** friends; I look back upon fifty years of **labor** spent here in defence of the truth—how **successfully**, and how much to the approbation of the **great Witness and Judge, another** day will tell— and I **find** that language **is but a poor** medium to convey a just impression of our mutual thankfulness and joy. And yet I have a filial wish **that cannot** be gratified, but whose gratification, if such a thing might be, would fill our cup till it should run over. I do not now so much advert to the painfully felt want of *her* presence, who, with your pastor, came among you in the days of her youth and loveliness, has shared with him these responsibilities, cheered him in many an hour of labor and lassitude, and **has** made his home—what the home of a minister should be, next to the pulpit—the dearest spot **on** earth. None who knew her can doubt that her genial spirit would respond to every grateful affection, which this occasion may well inspire. But my thoughts have been wandering to another negation, and I could wish, despite its impossibility, that the father and mother, who watched over your pastor's infancy, guided his youth, saw him inducted into the sacred office, and led to this large field of usefulness, and often blessed God that he permitted them to realize their fondest hopes concerning the son of their vows,—I could **wish, though nature** and providence almost alike forbid the utterance, that they **were** here to mingle their gratulations and thanksgivings with ours. But though they have long since joined the spirits of the just made perfect, we know the sentiments they would entertain, and what they would say, could their years have reached to this time. As their humble representative, let me give utterance to some of the thoughts which, were they here, they would **be** eager to express. I imagine I hear them say, "**We** received this our son from God, **and we gave him back to God. At** the baptismal **font, at the family** altar, **and** in our closets, this **dedication was** made **and** renewed. And it has been crowned with divine acceptance. We sought not for him temporal prosperity, the honor which cometh from men, official renown and popularity, nor even length of days, though all these have been vouchsafed beyond our expectation. We sought for him the presence of Christ in his work, success in gathering God's elect into his kingdom, boldness in declaring the whole counsel of **God, and a** cheerful **courage** as he should see the work of the Lord **prospering** in the hands of a mediator. And **all this and** more we have been permitted to witness. And for this we would ascribe the honor **where it is** due. It was not we, but the grace of God which was with us. We lay at the feet of the divine Saviour our tribute of acknowledgment of his mercy, and adore his matchless, condescending grace."

Something like this would be their sentiments, could they speak to us to-day. They were wont to ascribe all they were, and all their children were, **to the** rich and sovereign grace of the Most High. **And** what if their voice is not heard here, and what **if** it be an unsupported hypothesis that they even now know what is transpiring in this place of prayer—yet we know their spirit, and it is a spirit which children, who reverence their memory, may well cherish. One of them has left on record that she was "conscious of stronger actings of faith in God's covenant in the consecration of this son to him, than in the dedication of any other of her children;" and in the more vigorous, masculine mind with which she was associated in the parental work, there was a coincidence with these opinions **and** hopes. And I speak not my own sentiments **alone, but** those of two others, when I say, Let God have all the glory of what our elder and long revered brother is and has done. If he has "increased while we have decreased," **it** has been with the "increase of God." And if we can read his heart, there is not, amid all the memories and exultations **of** this day, one sentiment that takes the precedence of this, "Not I, but the grace of God which was with me." Your tribute, my friends,—his labors, more abundant than have fallen to the lot of most of the servants of our Master,—this rare completion of a life unusually favored,—he lays at the feet of the Crucified, with no more earnest or dearer wish than this, that "God in all things may be glorified through Jesus Christ."

At the conclusion of Dr. Spring's address, Rev. Dr. Rodgers, a grandson of Dr. John Rodgers, to whom Dr. Spring had alluded as having been the "Father of Presbyterianism in New York," arose and said:

ADDRESS OF REV. **DR.** RODGERS,

OF BOUNDBROOK, N. J.

Permit me, sir, to say how deeply grateful I feel to my venerated father and friend, Dr. Spring, for the proposition which he makes to his Session and Trustees, on behalf of my venerable grandfather.

I feel myself honored, sir, in having been invited to attend upon this delightful and interesting occasion. I regarded it as a high privilege to have been present when your venerated pastor delivered his half century sermon from **this desk, and to have** been permitted to take an humble part in the services of that long to be remembered **occasion.** I consider it a very great privilege to be present to take part in these services, as the representative of that venerated man to whom allusion has already been made as having been the instrument, in the hands of God, in founding the Brick Presbyterian church, in the city of New York. You will permit me to rejoice with you, sir, at seeing so many of the children of the Brick Church here to-night, while I regard myself as one of its grandchildren. My grandfather having been for so long a series of years its pastor, I am at any rate the grandchild of this church by *ecclesiastical descent*. Of very few of the churches, in this or any other land, can be said that which may be said of this old Brick Church,—that for ninety-three consecutive years it has never been vacant one hour, my grandfather having served this people as their pastor in the ministry of the gospel for forty-three years, and your present pastor having served for fifty years. It is true that Dr. Miller and Dr. McKnight were co-pastors with my grandfather for a number of years, but he was senior pastor of the church; and when Dr. McKnight retired, after the breaking up of the collegiate charge in 1809, Dr. Miller took charge of the Wall Street church. The Wall Street and Brick churches came forward and asked that they might be permitted to bear an equal proportion of the salary of that old minister who had so long served both churches, and that he might be regarded, to the end of his days, as their senior pastor. The deed from the corporation of the city of New York, granting that piece of land upon which the old Brick Church stood so long, was dated on the 5th of February, 1766. Soon after that deed was given, and that land came into the possession of the Presbyterian interest of this city, my grandfather went out and begged from door to door, as Dr. Spring has properly said, in order to the erection of the Brick Church, that there might be a second Presbyterian Church to accommodate the wants of the people in the upper part of the city of New York, and those who were living out of town. That was literally so, sir, for the Brick Church then stood almost outside the city of New York. On the 1st of January, 1768, the church having been built in 1767, my grandfather preached the dedication sermon from the text, "I will fill this house with glory, saith the Lord of Hosts." Sir, it was in the language of the Most High himself that that temple was dedicated to his service; and we all know,—those of us who can look back, for fifty years and over, upon the ministry of the gospel in that time-honored edifice,—we all know how gloriously that word was fulfilled in the outpouring of the Spirit, and the descent of its influences within that sacred temple. And we pray,— and the prayer is already granted to some extent, —that the same Spirit of the Most High God may fill this temple, and that the glory of the latter house may be greater than the glory of the former. Oh! should this declaration be fully accomplished, how glorious would be the dealings of Jehovah with those who worship here, and what reason would they have for exclaiming with adoring gratitude, "What hath God wrought!"

I have before me a record made by the Presbytery of New York, in the year 1810. At the meeting of the synod for that year, the Presbytery of New York sent up their statistical report, and this is a part of it: that they had "received under their care Mr. Gardiner Spring, a licentiate of the association of Westford, Mass., Aug. 7th, 1810, and that they had ordained Mr. Gardiner Spring to the work of the gospel ministry, and installed him pastor of the congregation worshipping in the Brick Church, New York, Aug. 8th, 1810." Reference has been made by Dr. Spring himself to the laying on of hands of the Presbytery upon that occasion, so solemn to him, and so delightful to those who were looking forward to his ministry. It was the last official act of my grandfather's life; it was the last ordination at which he attended.

Having laid his hands upon the head of his youthful colleague, and having asked for him the blessing of that God whom he had so long served, he retired from his labors; and soon after (it was in the next May) he entered into his rest. It is pleasant to me—very pleasant, I assure you, sir—

to meet this congregation here this evening. It is very pleasant for me to rejoice in all that I have seen and heard here; for you may well suppose, sir, that, my grandfather having been for so many years pastor of the Brick Church, I cannot but feel a deep interest in all that pertains to the prosperity of this congregation. **Most** heartily do I say, "Peace be within her walls, and prosperity within her palaces." And when this servant of God, **and** our brother who is standing by his side as his associate in the pastoral office, shall have passed away from earth to joys on high, and others come to take their places, may we not humbly hope that the remarks that have been made with reference to many who have been connected with the old **Brick** Church, may be made of **those** who shall worship here, of this one and that one, that they have been born unto God in Zion, and that this church may be perpetuated until the kingdom and dominion, and the greatness of the kingdom under the whole heaven, shall be given to the people of the saints of the Most High? Then, sir, shall come to pass the season when, in the language of one whom many of us loved, whose funeral sermon your pastor preached, by the side of whose grave your pastor wept—in the language of **the** sainted Whelpley:* "The **arch of** God's re-

---

* Mr. Whelpley was the pastor of the Wall St. church, and died while yet a young man. He was an accomplished scholar, and a very popular preacher.

deeming covenant shall **encircle these** bright heavens, and all nations shall rejoice beneath it."

Again I say, "Peace **be** within thy walls, and **prosperity within** thy palaces." "For my brethren and **my** companions' sake, I will now say, Peace **be within** thee!"

DR. HUMPHREY'S ADDRESS.

MR. CHAIRMAN:—For what my eyes have seen, my ears have heard, and my heart has felt in connection with this your sacred jubilee, I am indebted to the polite invitation **of** your committee, which has brought me **down from** my home in the hill country of **Berkshire to** rejoice with **you** this evening in your devout reminiscences and **thanksgivings** to the great Head of the church for **sparing to you the** life and labors of your now aged and always beloved pastor, from the budding of **the almond tree,** so full of promise, in this garden of the **Lord,** to its crown of glory in the fulness of its blossoms, **still** bringing forth fruit in its old age.

These scenes carry me **back** more than half a century, to the day when my friend and brother was the file leader of our class on the day of our graduation at Yale college. Thence we went out, not knowing whither we went. But, having obtained help of God, we continue unto this day.

To make the few remarks which I have to offer harmonize with the occasion, I cannot think of a more fitting theme than the *blessings of a permanent local ministry*. Time was, and a few of us remember it well, when pastors were settled for life. It was understood and expected that they were to live, and die, and be buried with their people. In those days of Puritan simplicity and continuance, dismissions were very rare. I remember but one within the whole range of more than thirty parishes, where I was brought up, till I had grown to manhood. A dismission was a very strange event, and much talked about. In those good old times it was not uncommon for ministers to preach fifty years and more in the same pulpit where they were first settled; and parishes might be named in which two ministers, in succession, labored, each, more than half a century. Nay, more. The records of some of the older churches will show that they have had three pastors, the aggregate of whose ministry exceeded *a hundred and fifty years!* When they could no longer go in and out before the people, by reason of age, colleagues were settled, to bear the burden and heat of the day; and when they died, "devout men carried them to their graves," followed by the lamentation of their whole flocks.

How great the change, within hardly two generations, to rotary arrivals and departures! Now, when a candidate receives and accepts a call, he does not expect to stay more than a few years at the longest; and the people regard it very much as they do any other temporary contract, liable to be dissolved at any time by mutual agreement, or rather, *without*, when either desires it. And, to make assurance doubly sure, it is often expressly stipulated in the contract, that by giving *three* or *six* months' notice, either the minister may leave or the people may send him away at any time. It is not so common now as it was some twenty-five years ago, and I suppose the main reason is, that the contract can be more promptly dissolved without any such stipulation than with it. It requires no six months' notice. If the pastor wishes to leave, he goes as soon as a Presbytery or a council can be called; or the people, when they choose, can send him away whether he will or no.

Indeed, it is becoming a serious question in many places whether it is best to go through the formality of installing and dismissing pastors at all; and so they resort more and more to what on the minutes are called *stated supplies*,—a convenient term of modern invention, which may mean hiring preaching by the year, six months, or any shorter time, at their option. This is about as far as rotation has **yet** gone in the progress of modern improvements. The next step must be to hire by the day as the farmers do, or to have no preaching at all. In the large cities, I know the pastoral care is in general more permanent; but even here it is a good deal disturbed by the rotary system.

Time will not allow me to discuss the question at any length, between permanence and rotation in the sacred calling; but I must crave your indulgence while I very briefly point out some of the advantages of the former over the latter. It takes time, in every profession and calling, to obtain the highest degree of influence and success. **Men** cannot, in any profession or responsible branch of business, break up often and remove from one place to another, without the danger of losing more than they can gain. It takes time to mature and carry out plans on which ultimate success essentially depends. It takes time, too, to gain friends and the widest personal influence. This is preëminently the case in our profession. **A you**ng preacher can't go and fully establish himself in any important parish **in** two or three years, or even in twice as many. He may be a first-rate preacher; he may be **all the** while gaining in the affections and confidence of his own people, and extending his influence into the surrounding parishes; but he cannot, except in rare cases, break up and change his location, without a great sacrifice of capital on which the power of the pulpit so much depends. He may go and settle somewhere else; (no, not *settle*,) but rent a house, or board out, with flattering prospects of usefulness; but he cannot carry his personal and ministerial influence along with him. In these respects he has got to commence, not where he left off, but where he began. He has got to form new acquaintances, and gradually rise in estimation and influence as before, instead of "going on unto perfection;" and by the time he is fairly up to the point which he had reached when he last struck his tent, the rotary system sweeps round and takes him off, without the trouble of rooting him up, and he goes forth once more to find a third location, if he can, where he may gird up his loins for another stage of his ministerial pilgrimage. In this manner not a few worthy pastors change their location *five* or *six* times; or, what is getting to be more common, before they are fifty years old they are set aside as quite too superannuated to keep up with the times.

And how can ministers grow up to full stature in their profession, under such a system? Why, it is very much like planting an oak, and pulling it up so often that it can take root nowhere, however rich the soil. Like the oak, the ministry wants a great many summers, and to stand a great many winters in one place, to strike its roots deep and spread its branches wide. I know there are exceptions. There are some wayfaring brethren in our profession, who, in spite of all their disadvantages, rise to high eminence and do a great deal of good; but this does not materially affect the general rule. Whatever may be said in favor of removals, 'few and far between," the present system of itinerancy, if persisted in, cannot fail, in the long run, to depreciate the ministry, and bring leanness upon the churches.

In striking contrast with this are the manifold advantages of the old system of permanent settlements. In those stabler times, as I have already remarked, when a young Timothy was ordained, it was a real *settlement*. It was understood **and expected,** on both sides, to be *for life*. **He looked upon** the flock as his permanent ministerial charge, committed to his watch and care by the chief Shepherd. And they received him as an ascension gift, not for two or three summers, more or less, but for life. He was *their* minister, and as they had no fears that some other parish would come and steal him away, they gave him their hearts at once. And he gave his **young** heart to them, as well as **his** time and services. However well the field might have been cultivated before he came, he saw there was more than enough left to tax **the best** powers of a much stronger man. He was under no temptation then to aim at immediate results, by novel measures and high pressure, at the expense of permanent religious usefulness. He felt that a life work was before him; that much depended upon him. He could take time to survey the ground thoroughly, and lay his plans for "making full proof of his ministry." He could look upon the children, not only as the lambs of his flock, but that, by feeding them with the "sincere milk of the word," he might nourish them up to bear strong meat, "that in due time he might bring them into the church, lean upon them in his declining years, and receive them as his crown of rejoicing in the day of the Lord Jesus!" Such delightful anticipations, a minister liable every year to be removed cannot indulge. How great the contrast, and how much in favor of a permanent ministry!

When a permanently settled pastor buries those who called him, their children, who have been trained up under him, naturally feel that it is their duty and their privilege to take their places, and sustain him. They have early attachments, which cannot be transferred to any stranger; and they will stand by him, when they might turn their backs upon any successor.

How great the advantage of a permanent over a shifting pastorate is, in point of *outside* influence, it needs not many words to show. Though of slow growth at first, it becomes a mighty power in a long and faithful ministry. It gives a force and weight to its opinions and counsels, which a long acquaintance only can secure. It is a sweet, pervading aroma, surpassing in fragrance every thing, save that in the song of songs, which is Solomon's.

And then, the outside influence which a good minister gains by remaining forty or fifty years in one place, hardly admits of calculation. Every body knows him, and knows where to find him. He is the father of the Presbytery;—that gets to be his title, with all the younger brethren, in the wide and widening circle around. They go to him for advice. They avail themselves of his treasured experience; they are helped by his counsels.

The churches, too, feel that **they have a father to go to in** their difficulties. In a word, by growing up with the people, identifying himself with their interests, and remaining through all the active period of life in the same place where he first settled, till removed by death, he accumulates a capital of ministerial influence which he could never have acquired by frequent removals.

If these views are correct, there must have been blame somewhere in bringing the present disturbing influence into pastoral relations. Where the blame lies, whether with the pastors or the parishes, or both, is a fair question. That some preachers may become uneasy, and seek for dismission without any good reason, we do not deny. But I feel bound to say, in behalf of our brethren, that many of them, especially in the larger towns, feel constrained to leave, when they would be glad to remain, if they could do all that is expected and required of them. They love their people, and the thought of a removal is a sore trial. But "necessity is laid upon them." They can't remain, as so much more is required of ministers now than there was fifty years ago, when comparatively little outside labor was called for; when there were no missionary, Bible, tract, and a great many other kindred societies to take care of—no collections to be taken up—no anniversaries to be attended—and very few ordinations and dismissions, to take up the time of pastors and wear them out. And then, too, satisfactory preparations for the pulpit did not cost near so much time and study as are now demanded, almost everywhere. People will have more popular and finished sermons, or they will not be satisfied. The young preacher knows it, and soon finds himself overtasked. His health fails in trying to keep up with the times; or, by taking care of it, work must be neglected, to the hazard of his standing in the estimation of his people. Under such circumstances, what can he do?

Many a pastor finds, early in his ministry, that he must do one of *three* things. He must *break down* early by overwork; or, by *favoring himself*, must *run* down, and lose his standing as a preacher; or, as the last resort, he must *leave* his beloved charge and try to find some other place, where he can avail himself of his previous hard work and experience. Will any one say that pastors so situated are to be charged with encouraging the rotation system by their example? The parishes, many of them, have "itching ears," that cannot long be satisfied with any one charmer, charm he never so wisely! Like the Athenians in Paul's day, they want something "newer" almost every Sabbath, and under the present uprooting system, they are quite as strongly tempted as the pastors are to seek for a change.

And now, dear friends of the Old Brick Church, I congratulate you that neither you, nor your present pastor, nor your fathers before you, have had any experience of the working of the rotation system, and have not desired to try it. Fifty years ago my brother came to you in the vigor and freshness of youth. You received him as an ascension gift, not only to yourselves, but your children. Without a break in the succession, he took up the mantle of that venerable father of the Presbyterian church, who lived to bury his generation, and by whom some of you were baptized. When "baptized himself for the dead," your now venerable pastor came at your call. He brought his heart with him into your pulpit and your families, and you gave him your hearts in return. "Having obtained help of God," he has gone in and out before you, till he has reached the latter part of the twelfth chapter of Ecclesiastes, with most of its infirmities light upon him, and is now able, with a vigor scarcely abated, to carry you back to the time when the dew of his youth was upon him, and to discourse upon all the way in which God has led you and him up to this hour. When he has been invited to leave you for other attractive fields of labor, his answer has uniformly been, "I dwell among my own people." Happy, thrice happy church! Congregations change. Those who bear onward the ark of the covenant grow old and die, but the church never.

Here you have now gathered, dear friends, to meet him "whom you have always delighted to honor, and to set up your Ebenezer." Well may you inscribe upon the monument, "Hitherto hath the Lord helped us." May he who dwelt in the bush still go before you. May he give you and the generations following pastors after his own heart, till you and they shall all be gathered with the general assembly and church of the first-born, whose names are written in heaven.

And now, in conclusion, my dear brother and classmate, I tender you my warmest congratulations, as to a spiritual father, revered and beloved by this great church and congregation. Highly favored of our blessed Master have you been, among his ministers. I cannot learn that, within the last hundred years at least, any one of his servants before you, in this great city, has ever preached half a century as you have done in one pulpit.

To hold the commission of an "Ambassador for Christ" a few years only, and to be found faithful, is an honor infinitely surpassing the highest worldly distinctions. How much more to hold the same commission for fifty years, from the highest Court in the universe, charged with such amazingly responible negotiations! To do this in one pulpit is an honor and privilege which I am afraid that not one in a thousand of our younger brethren can expect to enjoy. To "shine in courts," and be loaded with the highest rewards which royalty itself can bestow,—what is that, through the longest life, compared with "beseeching sinners, in Christ's stead, to be reconciled to God;" to be faithful unto death, and then, returning the commission to him who gave it, to go up and be "crowned with glory and honor and immortality in his kingdom!" Oh! after turning many to righteousness in this lower sphere, to be orbed, and "shine as the sun in the firmament, and as the stars, for ever and ever!" What a glorious galaxy of apostles and martyrs and other faithful servants of Christ will there be, shining brighter and brighter in those heavenly spheres, through all the revolving cycles of eternity!

While most of our class have gone to the dead, you and I, having obtained help of God, continue unto this time. I entered the ministry three years before you; but it has not been my privilege, as it has yours, to preach righteousness to one and the same great congregation for fifty years. I have labored as I could, by God's help, in two or three corners of our Master's vineyard. And it is somewhat remarkable, I think, that of the very few of our class that remain, *four* of the number, *Marsh* and *McLean*, beside ourselves, brethren beloved, in whom is no guile, have been in the ministry more than fifty years.

You, my brother, as well as we, have almost finished your course. You have kept the faith. You have instructed thousands. The ministers, when you came to New York,—the fathers and mothers of your own congregation and church,— where are they? You have lived to bury nearly two generations of your beloved flock. But their children and children's children, to "the third and fourth generation," have risen up to take their places, and call you blessed. The sun of your long day will ere long go down. It already gilds the evening clouds and sky. The earthly house of your tabernacle, though still in so much better keeping than mine, must, in like manner, be dissolved; and then, as you go up to take possession of the building of God, the house not made with hands, eternal in the heavens, methinks I see your best beloved here below coming to meet you at the golden gate, and surrounded, as you enter, by a glorious company, who are to be your "joy and crown of rejoicing in the day of the Lord Jesus."

ADDRESS OF REV. DR. MURRAY.

Mr. Chairman:—We may have a great many teachers, **but we can** have but one father;—so says the Sacred Record. We may be connected with many churches, **but** after all there is one church to which our affections always return, as the needle, which **has** been drawn from its true **direction, trembles back** to the pole. **I have been, in the course of** my ministry, acquainted with **many** ministers; **but** there is one minister who is associated with everything that is precious in my youthful years. I have been connected with many churches, but there is one church, in the aisle of which I stood when I devoted myself to God, and that church is ever before me. I came to this city, a mere boy, in the year 1818. **I** was, through the providence of God, cast into **a** Presbyterian family that worshipped in the Murray Street church, under the pas**toral** care of Rev. Dr. Mason, and I went there oc**casionally** to church. Dr. Mason was soon removed to the Presidency of Dickinson College, and on his removal, having no particular attachment there, save to hear the gospel **from** the lips of that eloquent man, I passed over the Park to the Old Brick Church. There I became acquainted with a few young men, one of whom still lives, a pillar of a church in Liverpool. We went into the Sabbath-school together. I was not then a professor of religion, but my mind became deeply interested, and **I had a** private conversation with Dr. Spring in reference to my state of mind, which was then in a very doubting state,—indeed, it was wavering as to the truth of Christianity itself; and he talked with me in the kindest manner. I called again: and I attended the lectures in that Old White Lecture-room in the evenings. At that time this beloved man, who has just been carried out to the Lecture-room (Mr. Holden*), was an elder. One evening Dr. Spring was unwell, and that man arose and read a sermon which I remember well; that sermon was from the text, "His feet stand on slippery places; **and** in due time they shall slide,"—a sermon in one of the volumes of the great Jonathan Edwards. It riveted my mind, and very deeply impressed my soul. I **went** again to see the pastor of the church, and he invited me to meet with the session, as it was my duty to become a communicant of the church. I went on a certain evening to meet with the session, and laid my hand upon the latch of the door in order to enter. But my heart failed me,

---

* Alluding to the fact of Mr. Holden having fainted during the exercises.

and I turned away. And for three months I stayed away. A notice was given again: I went to the same door and laid my finger upon the latch, but faltered, and was turning upon my heel to go away again, when that old and sainted man, Father Cunningham, came behind me, laid his hand upon the latch, opened the door, and said, "Walk in, young man;" and, almost against my will, I was ushered into the room,—where I went through such an examination as was usually there given, with a very faint heart. The following Sabbath I was received to the church. I was baptized by Rev. Dr. Spring in the name of the Father, Son, and Holy Ghost. By him I was led, in the private interviews to which I have alluded, to Christ; under his ministry I devoted myself to God; and by his hand I was baptized and received into the church. I went about my business. Six or eight months had passed away, when on a certain afternoon two individuals came into the office in which I was employed: one was Father Cunningham, and the other was another sainted elder of this church, years ago gone to rest, —Peter Hawes. They asked me, after a little introduction, if I thought of devoting myself to the ministry. I told them, No; that the thought had not entered my mind, and **that there were** other courses marked out before me. They told me to consider the subject, and that they would call to see me again. They saw me again: on a certain evening I had another conversation with them in the Lecture-room, and the result was that in a few months more I was in a course of preparation for the ministry, under the care of this church, and by advice of its pastor; and from that day unto this day, the Lord has kept me. Therefore, I ought and must feel a great veneration for this beloved man, and a great veneration for the Old Brick Church. I look around me this evening, and I find that many whose names have **been read** by our beloved Holden are absent: John Adams is gone; and Mr. Lockwood, and Peter Hawes, and Mr. Cunningham, and Mr. Phelps, and Mr. De Forest,—all gone! Mr. Fisher is yet living; Mr. Havens is gone; Mr. Couch yet lives; Mr. Holden has been here to-night; Halsey, too, is gone. Those men I knew as a boy; they were pillars of the church,—of the old house; they have fallen, but the main pillar remains.

It is one thing, Mr. Chairman, to **be a minister *in*** New York, and quite another thing to be a minister *of* New York. Almost any body with ordinary talent could be a minister in New York: John Smith could be a minister in New York—why, I myself could be that; but it is a very different thing to be a minister *of* New York. A minister *in* New York may **be a** very small minister indeed, and his ministrations may be very limited; but a minister *of* New **York** must be every inch a man. And this venerable man has been a **minister** *of* New York; his hand, for fifty years, has been upon everything that has been good here. What great and good enterprise has arisen here in this city for fifty years, with which his name has not been connected? **Is** it the Bible Society? is it the American Tract Society? is it any of our great missionary societies? And, if we go from our church to our national societies, is it the American Board? is it our own Presbyterian Board?—Pray tell we what it is that has arisen within the last fifty years in this city or in this land to bless the world, with which this beloved man has **not been** connected. **He** has been a minister, not only **in** and of New York, but he has been a minister of the world. His name is known in Ireland and in Scotland and in England, almost as well as it is known in the city of New York. His works praise him in the gate, and in every gate in the world. He has been a minister here, and a minister at the same time to our common humanity. Hence we should honor and imitate him. Not merely in the way that his venerable classmate (Dr. Humphrey) has stated, has he been a blessing, but in many **other** ways. He has been here for fifty years; the winds have beaten about him, and the floods have come up around him, but he has been **as a pillar,** unmoved. Why? Because, as a minister of Christ, as a preacher of the gospel, he has been founded on the Rock. Others have fallen and have been swept away, but he has remained strong and immovable as the mountains that surrounded Jerusalem. He has stood firm. Changes have passed over other churches and other men; clouds have passed over the characters of others, but the sun of this brother has shone clearly, summer and winter, for the last fifty years, and has been growing brighter and brighter and brighter, even unto the perfect day. Fifty years have passed over him,—and where in this city, or where in this land is the individual that can rise up and accuse him of saying any thing or doing any thing unworthy of his position as a Presbyterian minister of the gospel? Why, sir, in the presence of such a man I feel very much as one feels in one of those old cathedrals,—Westminster, for instance,—going around that old chapel of Henry VII.; or, standing under the shadow of those old trees in Hyde Park. I venerate those things; I look upon them with veneration; and we must venerate still more the man who, for fifty years, has gone on among the same people, preaching to them the truth, breaking to them the bread of life,—without a stain upon his character, and going down, quietly, the hill of life amid the admiration of those to whom he has so long ministered. Surely we must venerate such a man as that. But not in this way alone has he been a minister of New York. He has been a constant preacher, and, as I heard John Breckinridge say himself, one of the most impressive and eloquent men of his day, (and I repeat it now in his own presence,) the "prince of preachers." He has been not only a constant preacher, but he has been an industrious, laborious, and active man. He has made the most diligent preparation for the pulpit. He has brought out of his treasures things new and old, and has never drawn from the top of his mind, as a great many individuals do whose minds, unlike milk, make no cream. He gave them beaten oil from the sanctuary; and in this respect, as well in every other, he stands up before the youthful ministry of this land as a man in every way worthy of their imitation. If I, on a future occasion, should have any thing to say in reference to this man when his work is ended, I should hold him up to the ministry of this country as every way worthy of their respect and imitation. The course which he has pursued has made a man of him, and it would have made a man of an individual far less endowed by nature than he is. But the evening is becoming late. I feel that, as a son of this church, I could not say less than I have said.

There is one thing, however, that fills our hearts with mourning this evening, and that is, that the partner of his life should be absent from this ovation. But she has gone to a better and a higher world; and when her venerable partner goes the way which she has trod before him, if we live we shall strive to follow him to his resting-place, good men shall carry him to his burial, and long after his sun shall have set in the west, will its heavenly light shine on the high places of our Zion.

At the conclusion of Dr. Murray's remarks, the Chairman stated that, although there were other gentlemen present prepared to speak, men whom the audience would be delighted to hear, yet, as the hour was so late, and as it had been already announced that Dr. Hoge would "gather up the fragments," he would now call upon him to do so.

ADDRESS OF JOHN G. ADAMS, M. D.

MR. CHAIRMAN:—As one born into and nurtured in this church, and as the representative of the departed who, for a period of more than fourscore years, worshipped in this "holy mountain," I claim your indulgence for a few moments.

I ought to feel at home here to-night, sir, in this large congregation, for I may say, in the words of the divinely inspired poet,

"Here my friends and kindred dwell."

During my whole life has it been my privilege to

wait upon these ministrations; my whole history is identified with the history of this church, **and I come up here to-night, sir, to bear my testimony on** this most interesting occasion.

The memories of the past crowd upon me: I **recall** the services in the Old Brick Church and White Lecture-room—the Tuesday evening prayer-meeting—the lecture on Thursday evening—the instruction in the shorter catechism—the Bible-class —the singing-school—and the inquiry meeting;— I fondly cling to these memories; they can never be o**b**literated; they will abide with me forever.

I come to-night, sir, to bear my testimony to the faithful discharge **of** all the duties **of the sacred office by my venerable pastor, whose friendship it has been my privilege to enjoy during the entire course of** his ministry. In storm and in sunshine, **through** evil report **and** through good report, in times of depression, and under circumstances of great encouragement, in great infirmity of body, and in the fulness of his latter day strength, he has nobly fulfilled **his** mission. In the pulpit **on the** Sabbath, **at the** lecture and prayer-meeting during the week, **in his** visitation of the sick **and** dying, and in the last sad offices **for the departed,** he **has ever been the** faithful pastor, **the consistent** Christian, the constant friend. **With the** ideal of **the** great Irish poet,

"He has watched and wept, has prayed and felt for all."

He has not only "allured to brighter worlds," but by precept and example he has "*led the way*."

Tell me, Mr. Chairman, is not this "the highest style of man?" Once more, sir, I rejoice that I have been permitted to return to my native land in season for this most interesting occasion, and to offer up here, in this "second temple," my grateful tribute of praise and adoration.

May our venerated pastor be spared yet many years, to watch over this goodly heritage; and when the shadows of the dark valley close around him, may he be gently translated to the everlasting habitations prepared for all those who, having "finished their course with joy, do rest from their labors."

ADDRESS OF DR. HOGE.

WHEN brother Holden assigned to me, my friends, the office of "gathering up the fragments," he certainly gave me large latitude for a speech, and one rather alarming at this late hour, if you imagine the proportions of the ancient feast are to be observed: for there the "gathered fragments" greatly exceeded the unbroken loaves. I promise you it shall not be so now.

I think we have found it good to be here. The

house of God has been both solemn and cheerful. It has been a most pleasant scene. It has seemed like the evening of a long, fine summer day in harvest. The hours have been many, and warm, and full of honest toil; **but now** the west is golden, the air **is** dewy **and** full of balm, and we can look around over many a goodly sheaf of yellow grain. God bless the brave old reaper who has borne the burden and the heat of the day so long and so well; whose "hand has never waxed weary, nor his heart waxed **faint!**" Who does not envy him the song and gladness with which that harvest shall be shouted **home**?

Much of this harvest,—whose every grain **is a human** soul bought by the blood of God's **dear Son,** and "born of incorruptible seed, **by the word of** God, which **liveth** and abideth for ever,"—has **he** seen borne before him, from this field of earthly toil, to the heavenly treasure-house. For God has oftentimes sent His angels, and they have garnered now "the bearded grain," drooping with its precious weight, and **now the** "flowers that grow between."

Oh! friends, I behold two congregations to-night. I see *you*, with your warm hearts beating in love and gratitude to God, **and His servant, your spiritual** father and pastor. And though you have **assembled in** crowds, **your numbers** must be swelled by ministers of the gospel, **who** first heard **from his** lips the glad tidings they now preach to others; by elders, who were once of this membership, but are now ruling well, we trust, in sister churches; **and** by a host of brethren, who have gone out from your communion to the ends of the earth.

But "part of the host have crossed the flood;" **and can** you believe that they are not here to-night? **Are** we not still "One Church, above, beneath?" Aye, "**the** whole family in heaven and earth" is one. And as the mountain was full of horses and chariots of fire **round** about Elisha, which *he* saw, while his servant saw them not, till the Lord opened his eyes, but saw then with wonder and joy,—so, I doubt not, we are often surrounded by "the spirits of the just made perfect," and that it is but a thin veil which hides them from our eyes. And is it not thinner still to an aged servant of God, meet for his inheritance in **light?** "Though our outward man perish, yet the inward man is renewed day by day." Though the **eye of** sense grow dim, and look feebly on "the **things** which are seen," does not the eye of faith, **the eye of the** inward man, grow bright, under this gracious renewing, and look clearly on "the things which are not seen?" May not his hand almost reach theirs, and be grasped by their gentle palms?

Behold, then, gathering above his head, that infant throng, on whose brows he put the bright **seal of** covenant grace, and God so early set the crown of covenant glory. And there see those, who once came to him, wounded by the law, and with their "hearts choking them," as our brother **Murray** came; and those who hastened to tell, with joyous utterance, that they had "found Him of whom Moses in the law, and the prophets, did write, Jesus of Nazareth." There, too, with all who call him spiritual father, are all who, though "born" elsewhere, were "nourished and brought up" under his ministry.

And there I see that father and mother, whose words, coming to us through a brother's lips, we have heard to-night, as if they sounded from the upper Sanctuary; that godly father **and** mother, who consecrated him so fervently, and then trained him so diligently "in the nurture **and** admonition of the Lord," and now stand in thankful joy above him, and lay their hands in heavenly benediction on his head.

And is there not one more? Is *she* not here, who gave the dew of her morning beauty to his youth, and then walked by his side through a longer pilgrimage than the half century we are now celebrating; who, as she was the wife of his early manhood and his age through the kindness of God, was also, through His grace, the child of His ministry, his daughter in the gospel of Jesus Christ; whose unwearied energy and unfailing joyousness so greatly assisted and cheered his toils, and whose dying smile, from which the brightness was fading though all the sweetness was there, is now the dearest of earthly memories? Yes, she too is here, to bless him, and take her old place by his heart.

"It is a good sight," says Thomas Watson, "to see an old disciple; to see silver hairs adorned with golden virtues." That sight is, through the grace of God, before our eyes.

I have been constantly reminded, since my ministry has been mingled with that of your senior pastor, of the beautiful picture in the first Psalm: "And he shall be like a tree planted by the rivers of water, that bringeth forth his fruit in his season; his leaf also shall not wither; and whatsoever he doeth shall prosper."

As I came to this house to-night, and looked up to the clear sky filled with innumerable stars, I remembered, with solemn joy, that God had promised that "They that be teachers [so it is in the margin] shall shine as the brightness of the firmament; and they that turn many to righteousness, as the stars for ever and ever."

When the holy Rutherford was exiled from his beloved charge at Anwoth, and dwelt, "the Lord's prisoner," in Aberdeen, he cheered his drooping heart with the thought that if one soul from Anwoth should meet him at God's right hand, his heaven would be two heavens. Oh! my brother, my father, how many heavens, then, hast thou!

What shall I call thee? My colleague? That thou art by the solemn act of the church, ratified, I trust, in heaven. My brother? That thou art, **in** Christ, in the ministry, and in the love thou has shown me. My father? That, too, thou art, in age, **in** thy long pastorate, and in the reverence I owe thee.

I said, a little while ago, that this scene was like the evening of a fine summer day in harvest. I did not say the *close* of the day. The sun is descending indeed; but may He who heard the cry of his servant, "Sun, stand thou still upon Gibeon, and thou, Moon, in the valley of Ajalon," hear this **people's** prayer, and prolong the rich sunset, for our comfort and joy, through many a golden hour! May He permit us often to put in the sickle together! May He, indeed, make "the glory of this latter house greater than of the former," and permit your eyes to see it!

But I will not longer weary your heart. Amid all our joys this night, some gentle tears have fallen. But, **lo!** even

"The dews of sorrow are lustred o'er with love,"—

God's love, the love of the departed, **this** people's **love,** and last, though its worth be **least, my** own.

A TRIBUTE

TO

THE MEMORY OF A BELOVED WIFE.

A TRIBUTE

TO THE

MEMORY OF A BELOVED WIFE.

"Neither can they die any more: for they are equal unto the angels, and are the children of God, being the children of the resurrection."—LUKE xx. 36.

WE are not left to suspense and perplexity as to the existence and state of the human family beyond the grave. It is a dismal doctrine that the soul is *annihilated* when the body dies; it finds no countenance in reason or conscience, in nature or revelation. Nor is there a suggestion from reason or conscience, from nature or revelation, that the soul *sleeps* in the interval between death and the judgment. There is no such state of dreary solitude, no such incoherent and dreamy existence. The gospel holds out brighter prospects to the Christian's hope than this. The immaterial and immortal spirit within him lives, and shall never die: lives in an uninterrupted and glorious immortality. And thanks be to God, he has better prospects even than this purely spiritual and immortal existence. The resurrection of our Lord Jesus

Christ from the dead is the pledge that the whole being of his redeemed church, the body as well as the soul, the material as well as the immaterial, shall be presented at the Last Day, in a union for ever glorious and inviolable.

Such are the thoughts expressed in our text. When it declares, "Neither shall they die any more," the unavoidable implication is, that "it is appointed unto men *once* to die." The decree has gone forth, "Dust thou art, and unto dust shalt thou return." There is no discharge in that war. It is a condition of their existence, that they shall die. Ruthless, pitiless death is the destroyer of all; all indiscriminately, all promiscuously. All, of every class and clime, either now form, or will form the dust on which we tread. When from the sealed book the Lamb opened the fourth seal, the apostle "looked, and behold a pale horse, and his name that sat on him was DEATH, and *power* was given unto him." Kings and peasants fall alike before the ravages of this Destroyer. Slaves and conquerors are his victims. Nations are his subjects. Empires that alternately rose and fell, armies that filled the earth with noise and contention, navies whose thunder shook sea and land, cities whose business and bustle, whose laugh and song never thought of death, yield to his resistless sway. All that remains of them is the timeworn memorial that *they once were.* His are world-wide conquests; his standard a pall of sadness from the rising to the setting sun.

We are accustomed to speak of death as the law of nature, and as the debt of nature; but it is the law of God, the debt to justice. If man had never sinned, his body as well as his soul would have been immortal. He is mortal, not because he is God's creature merely, but because he is a sinner; not by the laws of his physical existence merely, but by the judicial sentence, "Death by sin." Death is God's decree for the sin of man. Men die as transgressors, bowing their head to the award that "death hath passed upon all men, for that all have sinned."

Why is it that the bed of death is so often the place of apprehension and suffering? Why, but that retributive justice there overtakes the sufferer, and he finds that "the sting of death is *sin?*" Other creatures die, but not as man dies. The lily of the valley droops, and the leaf of the forest fades. The lamb is led to the slaughter, and the eagle drops from his aerie without a thought of evil. Their death is not like man's. Sin has this condemning power.

The mystery of *life*, that active principle that pervades all animated existence, and binds them, however unlike, in one class—what is it? The man of genius and the idiot have this in common—that they live. And what invisible power, what almighty magnetism **is it** which causes inert matter to live, and move, and have a being; to respond to outward influences, to receive impressions from surrounding objects and mould them to its uses,—**itself** inert when once the unseen hand that sustains it is withdrawn? And if the mystery of life **is** wonderful, how much more wonderful is *the mystery of Death!* What an affecting transformation when vitality is departed, when the blight of death has crept upon that animated form, and when in an instant, from a thinking, sentient, active existence, it has become a clod, motionless, senseless, thoughtless! Draw aside the curtain from the couch where the stern messenger of God's justice is clasping its victim in its chill embrace. The spirit still lingers in its clay; the current of life still flows sluggishly on. But mark that panting breath, shorter and shorter to the last! It is a judicial infliction. The shadows are not now gathering; they are settled; the spirit is fled. This **is death.** Draw nigh where the being that we loved **once** lay, and view the form—*being* it is now no longer—that lies before you. We gaze—there is no **movement**; we speak—there is no answer. We kiss the brow—it is cold as **marble. We** press the hand—but there is **no** sign of recognition; it moves not from the place where death first laid it. This is death. The moth flutters about the candle we hold over the dead one's pillow, and in that little insect there is life; here, all is death. The soft breath that stirs that curl upon the cold brow has life; here, all is death. That which is not and never shall be death's, is gone. The face, so often lighted up with smiles, the eye that beamed with intelligence, the tongue that uttered counsels of wisdom, are gone. Stoop down and look into that new sepulchre just hewn out of the rock. All, all is mouldering to dust. It is locked up in the grave. Speak to it tones of sweet remembrance, or sobbing grief; chant over it the solemn dirge, and it hears not. That curious and complex mechanism which **for so** many years moved with such harmony and regularity, is broken. Pour upon it **the** concentrated shouts of a thousand battles, and it **wakes** not. Heaven's lightning wakes it not till the voice of the archangel and the trump of God call it to the Judgment. Yes, this is death. It it an affecting mystery in the government of the Most High; nor could we solve it, if it were not the award of justice for the sin of man.

"Once to die," is a lesson we all must learn. Whence this aversion to think of death, when the arrow to which our sins have given the sting may strike us without a moment's warning? **Whence** the strange stupidity that makes death **a** stranger, **when** we can scarcely leave **our own** dwellings without discovering some new avenue to the grave? **Oh!** how different would these Sabbaths be, and what different emotions should we bring to the house of God, if each of us felt that he must die!

But let us turn from this dark side of the picture—it has a brighter one. It would be the **extreme** of sadness to know this much of death if we knew no more. "If in this life only we have hope, **we are** of all men most to be commiserated." This **world would** be shrouded in gloom, if there were not a world where death never enters.

"Neither shall they die *any more*." Beautiful thought! "Whose wife shall she be of the seven?" was the question of the unbelieving Sadducees, in regard to the woman who, after having married seven husbands, herself died also. The Saviour's reply was, "Ye do err, not knowing the scriptures, nor the power of God. For in the resurrection they neither marry, nor are given in marriage." There will be no renewing of such earthly bonds there. There **will be** mutual recognition, and sweet memories, and joyous rehearsals of the way in which God has led them, **and** mutual loves; but it will be **love true** and **holy**, and like the love of God. It will embrace all, **and** receive the response of sympathy from all. **There** will be thoughts and emotions that are new because they are sinless,—emotions of admiration at bright forms **of beauty**; and as these beauties of holiness meet the eye, they will be the love, the admiration, the joy of heaven. There will be no unsubdued passions, no propensity to **evil,** no spirit of apostasy and revolt. No foe shall enter there; no serpent to sting, and no roaring lion going about seeking whom he may devour. It is a world of light,—the light of inviolable holiness; the light of eternal truth; themselves the elements of the pure river of the water of life, proceeding out of the throne of God and the Lamb. And because there is no sin, there is no pain and **no sorrow** there; no want to discourage, no anxiety **to** depress, no fear to agitate, no disappointment to break the heart. That last sigh, that last tear, that last breath that transmitted the living spirit to the land of immortality, closed its earthly history. **There** shall be no more wearisome days and **wakeful** nights; no more sad apprehension; no **more** anxious watching the symptoms of decay; **no** more counting of the heart's pulsations, and no more narrow inspection of the earthly fabric to see if its pillars do not tremble. There is no circle of mourners there. The pensive dirge, the solemn prayer, the funeral obsequies, this world of tears, this land of graves, are among "the former that are passed away." Death did its worst when it killed the body. That placid corpse is the **last of his** trophies. He has spent the last arrow in his **quiver.** His iron rod is broken; his power is **crushed**; the knell of his departure is sounded; and his own grave, deep and large, is at length dug in this his own empire of rebellion and **woe**, and no descending angel shall ever roll away the stone from the monster's sepulchre.

It is rather an illustration, an enlargement of these thoughts, than any needed proof of them, when it is added in the text, "for they are equal unto the angels, and are the children of God, being the children of the resurrection."

They are equal unto the angels. Angels are the most glorious of all created intelligences. They stood their probation, and were confirmed in holiness, progressingly "proving what is that good, and acceptable, and perfect will of God." St. Paul says of the redeemed church, "ye are come to an innumerable company of *angels*"—made like to them, pure spirits, themselves furnishing bright illustrations of the perfections of the Deity. Next to their perfect holiness, their noblest characteristic is their immortality. Once they were dying men; now, like the angels of God, they are "living ones." Time does not diminish their lustre, while the flight of ages adds to their intelligence and beauty. They dwell together in the same glorious mansions, are occupied in the same employments, and united in the same praise with the unfallen. It is a thought we scarcely know how to admit, much more to express, that when the souls of believers pass from the pillow of death to their reserved inheritance, they attain to this angelic dignity and glory. Yet we cannot mistake the Saviour's declaration in the text, when he affirms, "They are equal unto the angels." **From the** low service of this poor earth, where their views are so partial and obscure, their sanctified and their unsanctified nature in such collision, and their moral imperfection so interrupts them in doing God's will, they shall become kings and priests unto God, "swift to do his will, hearkening to the voice of his word." From the pupilage of earth they shall pass to the "stature of perfect men in Christ Jesus," and their work and service shall be worthy of their manhood. Differ they do, and differ they will, as the redeemed infant differs from the redeemed parent, as the converted thief differs **from** the sainted Paul, as "one star differeth from another star in glory;" but all reflecting the bright rays **of** the Sun of Righteousness, luminous in his light, glowing with his beauty. Oh! the infinite love and condescension of the Eternal One, to admit such worms into such sympathies and fellowship, and to have the same access to him which Gabriel has, who stands in the presence of God!

To this representation the Saviour adds, *for they are the children* ***of God***. That they are the children of God by faith in Jesus Christ; **that they are** adopted into the divine family, **and** have a right to all the privileges of **sonship**; that he is a father to them, and they his sons and daughters; **and that,** by virtue of their union to Christ as the elder brother and kinsman Redeemer, they are "heirs of God, and joint heirs with Jesus Christ, are undoubted truths and unspeakably precious. Yet we cannot but regard the phrase "the children of God," in the connexion in which it stands, as designed to be exegetical of the words "Neither shall they die any more." The special import of it would seem to be, that, as the children of God, they are partakers of the divine nature—the deathless nature of God himself. Is He immortal? so are they. Will He exist eternally? so will they. Here, they were creatures of yesterday: some terminated their existence in the cradle, some in the vigor of manhood, some in the decrepitude of age. There is an eternal duration, stretching on, onward for ever. We bury our dead out of our sight, not so fully and joyfully instructed as we ought, that they still live in the unbroken series of interminable ages. In this world they were in a state of exile; beyond, they have come home to their Father's house. They dwell in his high and holy place, and inhabit eternity. I have stood by the dying-bed of multitudes who feared God and loved his Son. I have sighed at their last sigh. I have strewed flowers upon their sepulchre, and wept with those who wept as we turned away from the rock that covers them. But when, by the eye of faith, I beheld that immortal spirit soaring in its flight, I could not but congratulate the departed that

they had broken the doors of their prison-house, gained the victory, and begun their everlasting song.

The text also subjoins another thought: "they are the children of God, *being the children of the resurrection.* This is the crowning reality, that they are the children of the resurrection. The resurrection of the body rests upon the resurrection of the body of Jesus Christ from the tomb of Joseph of Arimathea. The *fact that he died* is a fact recorded in history; and the fact that *he rose from the dead on the third day,* is also a purely historical fact, **proved by** recorded testimony. But **the** fact that "*he died for* our sins and *arose again for our justification*" is a great *doctrine* which **all Christians receive on** the testimony of God himself.

The remark deserves consideration, **that the** work of Christ on the earth was not completed until he rose from the dead.* He bore our sins in his own body on the tree; they were upon him when he died. The burden sunk him to the dust of death; nor did he throw it off so long as he lay in the grave. **He** continued under the power of death for a time; **and** if he had never risen, **he** would have continued under the burden of our sins. If he had not risen, his people would never have risen. Hence the apostle declares, "If Christ

---

* See a work by Dr. Candlesh, of Edinburgh, entitled "Life in a *Risen* Saviour."

be not risen, then is our preaching vain, and your faith is also vain; ye are yet in your sins."

In that wonderful chapter, the fifteenth of his first Epistle to the Corinthians, in which he speaks of the resurrection of the redeemed, he lays **the foundation** of his argument upon the historical fact **that Christ** rose from the dead. His proof is, **that** Christ's resurrection is predicted in the Old Testament: he **rose** " again the **third** day, *according to the scriptures.*" He then goes on to **say, that** he appeared after his resurrection, first to **Peter,** then to the twelve, then to upwards of five hundred brethren at once, and last of all to **St. Paul** himself, as to one born out of due time. What historical event is established on surer evidence? To deny it is to subvert the gospel, make its **author** and its preachers false witnesses, and **destroy the** faith and hopes of all the people of **God.** Never were witnesses more **competent, more intelligent and** informed, more disinterested **and self-denying, than the** witnesses of Christ's resurrection. **Their constancy** subjected them to privation, infamy, and death; **while** the contumely, persecutions, and suffering entailed on them by it had **no** respite but in the grave.

If, then, Christ **rose from the** dead, his people will rise.* " As the first Adam secured the death

---

* For a happy illustration of this argument, see Pool's Annotations and the Commentary of Dr. Hodge, in locis.

of all who are in him," so the "second Adam secures the life of all those who are in him." When his body was reunited to his soul, then his work was complete. Not until the chains of death were broken was he free. And not until he was thus completely rid of the curse, could the deliverance of those who believe in him be looked for as glorious and complete. It is because he rose that their triumph is sure. When the soul and the body, separated at death, are reunited at the resurrection, the condemning sentence, "the soul that sinneth shall die," is completely reversed. In his triumph, the bodies of his saints are not forgotten; for "those who sleep in Jesus will God bring with him." His resurrection is a pledge of theirs; for he is "become the *first fruits* of them that slept." They look for it, nor will they look in vain. What his resurrection secured for him, that it secures for them. They are under the power of death for a time, as he was; and as he is, now that he is risen, that they are to be. "When he shall appear, they also shall appear with him in glory." They are his body, the fulness of him that filleth all in all. "It is his body that lies wherever his buried saints lie; nor will his resurrection be complete until they rise in him." It was a pensive chamber where they breathed their last; the death-struggle was severe. It is a cheerless house,—that cold, dark vault; and the slumber of the grave seems long.

But at his coming who is the resurrection and the life, he shall take them to be with him, and "their resurrection shall be the complement of his own." Away in some bright orb of light he shall gather his saints together, those who have made a covenant with him by sacrifice, where they "shall not die any more, for they are the children of God, being the children of the resurrection."

And is not this delightful truth confirmed by a thousand analogies of nature? The light of the sun fades and dies, and the children of men, worn with toil, lose their active existence in sleep and darkness; again, the day dawns, the darkness is past, and they awake to newness of life. The moon wanes and dies; and then, with the regularity of nature's great chronometer, its faded glory is restored. Look first at the vegetable creation. Cold winter wraps in its icy winding-sheet the departed year; and forests and fields and harvests all fade as a leaf, and lie buried in the tomb. But at the vernal breath of the returning year, all nature comes forth refreshed from the sleep of the grave, and shouts for joy. And is there no resurrection? Is it so, that death chills and freezes for ever the current of human existence? Shall that cold clay bloom no more? and that eye never more beam with lustre? and no voice be ever again heard from those lips that moulder in the tomb?

> "Shall life revisit dying worms,
>   And spread the joyous insect's wing;
> And, oh! shall man awake no more
>   **Thy face to** see, thy name to sing?"

No: it is not in vain that we wander along **the** shores of that unseen world. A sound does reach us from this vast abyss of waters. Earth and sea shall give up their dead.

But *how* are the dead raised up? The men of Grecian culture asked the question, "*With what body* do they come?" St. Paul thought it a foolish question; and **his** answer is substantially as **follows**: When we look beneath us, around **us, above us, we see** material substances **in untold varieties and** modifications, throughout **the vegetable, animal, and** stellar creation.

Look first at the vegetable creation. "That which thou *sowest* is not quickened **except** *it die;* and that which thou sowest, thou sowest not that body that shall be, but **bare** grain: it may chance of wheat, or some other grain. But God giveth it a body as it hath pleased him, and to every seed his own body." If then "the grain you cast **into** the earth cannot **live** and bring forth fruit *unless* it die, is it not absurd to say, the **body** cannot live *because* it dies? **You** plant a **seed, but** it does not come up a seed, but a flower. **Why** then may not **the future be** to the **present** body what the flower is to the seed?" From the vapors of the sea and the miasma of the slain on the field of battle, arise the beauty, the brilliancy, the glory of the western sky; and from the sand of the ocean's bed, and the charcoal of the forest, come forth the crystal and the diamond. And why, from this natural and corruptible body which sleeps in the grave, may there not come forth a body that is spiritual and incorruptible?

Turn your thoughts then to the animal world, and you see the same varied modifications. Flesh and blood appear in a great variety of forms: "there is one kind of flesh of men, another flesh of beasts, another of fishes, and another of birds." Mark the insects which move on the surface of the ground, or swim in the deep sea. They build their sepulchres, and seem to be dead and dissolved in dust. Yet these lifeless insects rise in forms of beauty, "dance in the air, sleep on flowers, and feed on honey and dew." The silkworm, at first a speck of matter scarcely visible to the naked eye, spins its own shroud, and enwraps itself in its own silken robe and dies; and then bursts its prison and comes forth a new creature, in a gorgeous dress, and to live in a new world. And do not these transformations favor the thought that we may rise in a body more glorious than that which was deposited in the grave?

Look now at the celestial bodies. "There are celestial bodies and bodies terrestrial; but the glory of the celestial is one, and the glory of the terrestrial is another. There is one glory of the sun, and another glory of the moon, and another glory of the stars; for one star differeth from another star in glory." We know not the elements of which these heavenly bodies are compounded; but they are material bodies, and more glorious modifications of matter than the elements which form the seed you cast into the ground, or the reptile that crawls upon it. And if what you sow is not that which you reap; if the meanest worm is not the splendid tenant of the air; if matter exists in unnumbered forms, from the decayed vegetable to the stars and the sun in the firmament,—why, when the grave receives a natural and corruptible body, may it not yield a body that is spiritual and incorruptible? There is a great change from the infant in its mother's womb, to the full grown man; yet is it the same creature of God, and has the same conscious identity and accountableness. So there is a great change from the corruptible body that is deposited in the grave, to the incorruptible at the resurrection. "It is sown in corruption," enfeebled and corrupted by disease, subject to decay, and **not unfrequently** in part dissolved before the tide of life ceases to flow; and destined to **dissolve in** rottenness and dust. The form, once so fair and beautiful, is shrouded in darkness, and hurried away from the abodes of the living. But "it is raised in incorruption," reproduced and reëmbodied, never again to be invaded by infirmity or disease, but to bloom in the regions of a living immortality. "It is sown in dishonor;" and, though once sparkling in the cheerful circles of time, is now despoiled of its attractiveness—its loveliness fled, its lustre gone, and a place assigned to it where the worm feeds, and from which the eye turns away. But "it is raised in glory;" its ignominy is wiped away in the grave. It rises in beauty and splendor, and is fashioned "like unto Christ's glorious body." "It is sown in weakness." Nothing is more weak. It is powerless. It is a mere inert, lifeless corpse; a skull, a skeleton, a mass of motionless dust. But "it is raised in power;" its sprightliness and activity all restored, revived in more than youthful vigor, instinct with energy, endowed with faculties of which we now have no conception, "always new and ever young." It is "sown a natural body;" a body of which mere animal life is the animating principle; a body consisting of flesh and blood, and sustained by air, food, and rest; a mere animal body, adapted to the condition of a mere earthly existence. And "it is raised a spiritual body." We know not the nature of spiritual bodies. We can only say, they are bodies of which something beyond animal life is the animating principle. It is a body, the animating principle of which is the soul,—the rational, immortal principle of our nature. It is a spiritual body fitted for the residence of the perfected spirit, for a spiritual service, a spiritual eternity. In form, in conscious identity, it will be the same body that lived on the earth and was deposited in the grave. It is the same body that is born that dies, and the same that dies that shall rise again. It is no new creation; it is a resurrection of the same body. *This* corruption shall put on incorruption; *this* mortal, immortality. All the examples of a resurrection,—the body of Christ, and the bodies of those who came out of their graves at his resurrection,—confirm the conclusion THAT THE SAME BODY RISES THAT DIED. But while **they** retain their essential identity, oh! how changed! The chaos and darkness which inhabited the grave **will** then be lighted up into life, light, order, and beauty. It is a privilege to live, a privilege to die, thus to rise. There is a no more gloomy and affecting spectacle than that which is presented in the mansions of the **dead**; and none more glorious than that which will be presented on the morning of the resurrection. **When** the night of death shall have passed away, what spot on the face of this globe will present to enraptured admiration **a view so** grand and beautiful as some densely **populated** graveyard!

You and I shall be witnesses **of** that wondrous transformation. The pomp of worldly grandeur, the glitter of worldly wealth, the refinement of worldly pleasure, will soon have passed, and the last of days will dawn. And, oh! what scenes of grandeur and beauty will then be presented to the astonished, the enraptured eye! What amazing scenes, when, as this earth revolves in its last diurnal circuit, the knell of a departed world shall have been sounded; when "the living shall be changed and the dead shall be raised;" and all that are in their graves shall hear the voice of the Son of God, and come forth! From lands and seas, from every river, every cavern, from the sultry desert, from the polar glaciers, aye, from the ambient atmosphere, where the dust of martyrs rose in fire and smoke and vapor, and was blown abroad to the winds,—all shall come forth, until the compact soil itself, crowded with the bodies of the dead, rises above the rock-ribbed skeleton of an expiring world. What an appalling spectacle to the awe-struck universe, when those celestial spirits who witnessed the primeval creation, now witness its final consummation! Then the history of mortal man, of time, will be finished; death shall be swallowed up in victory, and the book closed and sealed for ever. Glorious truth—" neither shall they die any more; for they are equal unto the angels, and are the **children of God**, being the children of the resurrection!"

After the scenes that have recently taken place in the midst of us, and the kind references to the beloved woman so recently taken from us, it may seem to some that enough has been said on this mournful theme. I may be allowed, however, to say, that I owe it to this church, to which she has usefully sustained the delicate and responsible relation of the pastor's wife; I owe it to her children, to her character, to my own heart, to her God and my God, to avail myself of the present opportunity in paying a brief tribute to the memory of one who has so long been my solace in the labors of this ministry.

She was a native of the city of New Haven, in the state of Connecticut, and was born on the first of September, 1785. In her person, she was beautiful to the last; in her youth, very few were more attractive. She had a fine intellect, combining clear conceptions, strong reasoning powers, a warm heart, a lively and poetic imagination, keen wit, abounding pleasantry, and a memory that rarely forgot any thing she had read, heard, or seen. Her mind was cultivated by extensive reading, and especially in the departments of biography and history. Her colloquial powers were of a rare order, and attractive to all classes. No matter what their station in life, she had a word in season for all; few, if any, ever spent a leisure **hour** in her society without recalling it with pleasure. In her youth and in her maturity, she was a magnet to the young, enjoying their pleasures, elevating their character, and promoting their usefulness. Children loved and sought her society, even in her old age.

A prominent feature in her character was her *cheerfulness*. She was rarely pensive; and when she was so, it was touching pensiveness, and among the most affecting expressions of female loveliness. But it was a rare occurrence, even in a life protracted thus long, and so chequered with trials. How often have I wished that I could look on the bright side, and with the same sunshine of the mind with which she was favored! In this particular she was the charm of our domestic circle, shooting her beams of pleasantry like golden threads through the web of social life, infusing vivacity into its toil, giving tranquillity to its apprehensions, alleviation to its sorrows, and brightness to its joys. Her life, as I look back upon it, though one of incessant care and labor and responsibility, was, to an unusual degree, a happy life. She enjoyed it; and never more than when others enjoyed it with her. Nor may I suppress the thought, that the cheerfulness she threw around those chambers of sickness where she was so often a sufferer, and especially her last sickness, was perfectly beautiful. It was a rich treat to sit hour after hour by her bedside; and while we saw that fair flower droop and gradually wither, we felt that its fragrance was exhaled from every decaying leaf. Something bright, something encouraging, something charged with the fulness of her own hoping, cheered heart, was every now and then playing **upon** her features, or flowing from her lips.

She was married on the 25th of May, 1806. We lived together four and fifty years; and our attachment, mutual and ardent in youth, was strong and sweet to the end. God was pleased to give us a large family, nine of which remain and six have fallen asleep. I had no friend on earth on whom I had such reliance; no counsellor so wise, and no such comforter. Her discriminations of character were remarkable, and rarely was she deceived in **them.** Her good judgment and practical **common** sense might almost always be relied **on.** We have **rarely** differed in opinion in matters of **any** importance; and when we did, I generally found in the end that she was right and I was wrong. Her practical wisdom was felt **also in all** those minor domestic arrangements, and those fitting adaptations of persons and things to times and places, which secure the greatest efficiency with the least interference. Matters like these may seem of trivial moment to those who are born and nursed in affluence; but in a long series of years they are serious matters, especially in a wife of a minister of the gospel.

She was eminently a self-sacrificing woman. She had no earthly object so dear to her as her husband's usefulness and honor as an ambassador of Christ, and the spiritual and temporal prosperity of her children. To me she was an affectionate, watchful, self-denying wife; to them an affectionate, watchful, self-sacrificing mother. Her husband and her children can bear witness that she preferred their interest and happiness to her own. I could state not a few touching instances of this self-devotement, were it proper to do so. By day and by night, at home and abroad, in sickness and in health, in prosperity and in adversity, and in all her pecuniary arrangements, I have never known, in all my ministry, her own convenience, or comfort, or pleasure stand in the way of my duty to God and this people. Would there were more such women, in this strong and beautiful feature of her character! An aged brother in the ministry, who had long known her, and knew her well, very soon after her death wrote to me as follows: "In your sorrow I know you have abundant consolation. May God multiply it even more; and to you and your children may it bring forth its ripest fruits! As a minister's wife, I have long felt that the departed one was a model. Not one rare excellence, but many, qualified her to be the light of your house, and a blessing to your people. You have lost much. But I know you thankfully remember that you have long enjoyed the precious gift, and that you appreciate the privilege of having had so much to lose." A lady of our own church, a long-tried friend, very kindly sent me the following testimonial: "The impressions Mrs. Spring made upon me in my interviews with her were of the pleasantest character. They were that she possessed rare and social qualities; a strong and cultivated mind; was an intelligent, well-informed, and mature Christian,—devoted to you and to the interests of the church of which God had made you overseer. Few, if any, interested me more than your departed wife; and I always esteemed it a privilege to be admitted to her society."

Of her *religious* character I can speak with thankfulness. We were neither of us the professed followers of Christ at the time of our marriage. The third day after our union, when on a tour to visit my parents, and the wedding-party which had accompanied us from New Haven to Hartford had separated from us, and we had retired to our chamber, we kneeled together for the first time in prayer. I never shall forget the hour, nor the place. It was in a comfortable hotel, and in the quiet village of Longmeadow, in the State of Massachusetts. And need I say, that from that hour we felt bound together by new bonds of affection and confidence. It was the commencement of our family worship, and was continued and daily renewed to the evening before her death. She did not make a public profession of her faith in Christ until seven years after her marriage, and three years after she came to New York. But she did it intelligently, and with clear views of God's truth and her own duty. Christ was her refuge. She came to him humbly, but cheerfully; with nothing but her sins for him to forgive, and nothing but her wants for him to supply. Her religion was made up of strong principles; devotement to duty; implicit confidence in the Deity, the atoning sacrifice, and justifying righteousness of the Son of God; a stern attachment to truth and right; modest, but sometimes sarcastic rebukes of wickedness; and a life of unostentatious and joyous consecration to higher interests than her own. There was no severity, no gloom thrown around the truths, the privileges, the obligations of the gospel where her influence was felt. Yet there was no lightness, and no reluctance to urge its claims. In those outpourings of the Spirit of God upon this people which form the brightest pages of our history, she was greatly useful among her young female friends. So *accessible* was she, that they often resorted to her; nor are there wanting, among the living and the dead, those who are witnesses of her sympathy and judicious counsels. She was not forgetful to entertain strangers, especially during the earlier part of her history; and, if I mistake not, she will be long remembered by those ministers of the gospel who enjoyed her hospitality. In her attachment to the Shorter Catechism of the Westminster Assembly, and in her painstaking efforts to imbue the minds of **her children with its truths,** she was a true **Puritan** mother. She was **a lover of the** Bible. She had great reverence for it, and read it much; **and,** though the best of commentaries were within her reach, she preferred to read it without note or comment,— comparing scripture with scripture. The Bible was her standard. "How readest thou?" was a question not only familiar to her own mind, but one with which she often troubled self-conceited controversialists. **She had no desire to be " wise above** what is written;" and would often **say of** certain new systems, and certain classes of men and *women*, "They do err, not knowing the **scriptures, nor the** power of God."

Those who knew her only during the last few years of her life, *did not know her*. For two years before her death she was a sufferer; **not so** much through pain as increasing debility. Yet these two years were years not of morbid melancholy, but of undiminished cheerfulness. The last few months of her life forbade **all hope of her** recovery. She saw her end approaching, and awaited it with submission and hope, expressing only the wish that she might be spared until the approaching fiftieth anniversary of my ordination. And she did live *eight and forty hours* after that memorable and painful Sabbath. She had learned to bow her will to the will of God.

The most painful thought I heard from her lips was, "Oh! *I am a crushed worm!*" As I one day held her in my arms, she remarked, "It is very pleasant for me to feel that I lie here in the hands of God." Then, after a moment's pause, she added, "I know of no thought more sweet, unless it be some bright views of the way of salvation by Jesus Christ." I asked her if the truths of the gospel appeared as *realities* to her own mind. She replied, "*Of course they do.*" I asked her again if she took hold of them as *strong* truths, and if she rested her eternity upon them. Again she answered, in her own pithy language, "*Of course I do.*" It was the custom of our dispersed children to meet in their mother's chamber every Saturday evening. About a fortnight before her death, and while she lay so enfeebled that we did not know she would notice the reading, I read to them the discourse lately delivered to you, entitled "Redemption God's greatest work." We did not know that she heard a word of it; but, at the close, she audibly exclaimed, "Glorious Redemption! glorious Redemption!"

She was fond of music; she read its language easily, and her sweet voice in sacred song gave sweetness to our daily worship. We all sang with her; and when she could no longer unite with us, she would select the hymns for us to sing. Very often the stanzas were from the hymn—

> "I'm a pilgrim and I'm a stranger;
>   I can **tarry** but a night:
> Do not **detain** me, for I am going
> To where the fountains are ever flowing,
>   And my Redeemer is the light."

On another occasion it was—

> "Jesus, lover of my soul!
> Let me to thy bosom fly,"

in the beautiful but neglected tune of Hotham. On other occasions it was—

> "Just as I am, without one plea,
> But that thy blood was shed for me,
> **And** that thou bid'st me come to thee,
> **O Lamb** of God, I come, I come!"

Our evening worship **was** always in her chamber; and on the evening **of the** Lord's Day she almost uniformly selected that beautiful hymn of Watts,

> "Father, I long, I faint to see
>   The place of thine abode;
> I'd leave thine earthly courts, and flee
>   Up to thy seat, my God!"

Ten days before her departure, her debility was extreme; and we never retired for the night without the apprehension of being called to her bedside before morning, to **see her die**. On the **evening of the last Lord's Day but one before she died**, we were singing the **hymn**,

> "My God, the spring of all my joys,
>   The life of my delights,
> The glory of my brightest days,
>   And comfort of my nights,"

when, wonderful to us all, as we were rehearsing the words,

> "The opening heavens around me shine
> With beams of brightest bliss;
> While Jesus shows his heart is mine,
> And whispers, *I am his*,"—

we heard her feeble voice uniting with us. Little did we expect ever to hear that voice of praise again this side of heaven; but, as we came to the words,

> "My soul would leave this heavy clay
> At that transporting word,"

that loving voice which had so often charmed us broke forth in heaven-imparted energy, and she sang—

> "Fearless of hell and ghastly death,
> I'd break through every foe;
> The wings of love and arms of faith
> Shall bear me conqueror through."

They were her last words; it was our last song on the earth.

This was on Sabbath evening. On the following morning there was a partial paralysis of her right side; very obviously her life on the earth was drawing to its close. She could not speak distinctly after this. Her mind was still clear, but she could converse with us only by the expression of her countenance and the pressure of her hand. We were exceedingly anxious that God would grant her the power of speech to the last; but in this our prayer was **denied. Yet she** did not leave **us** without some delightful witness of her faith, and hope, and joy. It was a week of trial, such as I hope never to see again. Yet was it a most delightful week to her and to us **all**: so full of sweetness, that it seemed to me it was given to *us* as the sweetest alleviation of our griefs—to *her* as an earnest of her **heavenly** rest. She knew us all until about **two days before she died;** during which **she** was unconscious. **Yet was it a great comfort to us to sit by her, and look on that calm** and heavenly face. **On the morning of the 7th of** August, at half **past** eight **o'clock, she was** released from debility and suffering, **and entered** her Father's house. **She** died **in the** presence **of** her husband and her eight children, and **her** attached nurse and servants, all of whom ministered **to** her with constant **and** unwearied **care, and great** love and tenderness. She was buried in a **vault** beneath the tower of **this** church, **where** she herself had once intimated that it would be a pleasant resting-place, by the side of her husband, until the resurrection.

I bless God for **a** helper so meet and fitted to **my** character and toils as a minister of the gospel. **I** bless him that he gave her to me, and that I had her so long. I bless him that I had so much joy in my attentions to her during her prolonged illness, and so many tokens of her love. And, although these pages are not written without tears, I bless him that her course is finished, and that her aching head is at rest. I bless him that, through him who loved us both, she has gained the victory and wears the crown, and that at the resurrection of the just I shall see and recognize that dear form again. I watched her last breath, and could not but congratulate her that the former things are passed away. Oh, fairest flower! bleak winter has but embosomed thee in his snow-soft arms, to bloom afresh in the Paradise above. Never did I appreciate the Christian doctrine of the resurrection until I deposited beneath yonder tower the mortal remains of the woman I so much loved. There they sleep; that church-going bell telling of her departure, that lofty spire her monument. There she sleeps, but only "till the heavens be no more." Believe me, there are joys in the assured anticipation that " all that are in their graves shall hear his voice and come forth," which none but mourners know. I marvel not that the New Testament magnifies it; nor that the harp of ancient seers should strike the note, "Awake and sing, ye that dwell in dust! for thy dew is as the dew of herbs, and the earth shall cast out her dead."

There is a touching incident in the divine record, in regard to the "father of the faithful," which has emboldened me, on the present occasion, to throw myself on your indulgence. It is in the following words: "And Sarah died in Kirjath-arba; the same is Hebron, in the land of Canaan; and Abraham came to mourn for Sarah, and to weep for her." I may be allowed, my beloved people, to solicit an interest in your prayers for a sanctified improvement of a like affliction to my own soul, to our dear children, and to this congregation. I ask them for myself, that my grief may be neither discontent, nor despondency, nor defiance, nor despair; but tranquil submission and humble self-abasement under God's chastising hand. I think of coming solitude and sorrows, and feel that I need *her* to encourage and comfort me. I think of surrounding mercies, and the increasing tokens of your favor, and say, What are they all without *her?* I can not look to earth; clouds darken on my pathway now.

Ere long, they will obscure your pathway as well as mine. These earthly ties must all be sundered. What you need is a well-grounded hope of a holy and blissful immortality; that, when the day of adversity comes, you " sorrow not as those who have no hope;" and, when death approaches and the grave covers you, you and those who **love** you may have the joy that you sleep in Jesus. Life is a blessing so long as we live to life's great end. It is worthless but for this; it is the happiest life even **amid life's bitter sorrows. Death too is** a blessing when our work is done: it delivers from sins, and conflicts, and sorrows, and terminates in joys known only to the spirits of just men made perfect. We die, and sleep in the dust; but over those who thus sleep intervening ages will pass rapidly away. There is no dial-plate there on which to count the hours of time. The busy world of life, which wakes at each morning and ceases every night, goes on above them; but to them all is silent and unseen. The greetings of joy and the voice of grief, the revolution of empires and the lapse of ages, send no sound within that narrow cell. The inscription upon their monumental marble tells the centuries that have passed away; but to the sleeping dead the long interval is unobserved. Everlasting thanks to the God and Father of our Lord Jesus Christ, it is but a short winter's day between the period when the eye is closed in the grave and when it wakes at the resurrection. "Behold, he cometh in clouds, and every eye shall see him!" You will awake and be there, my hearers, and so shall I. And so will the loved ones we have buried out of our sight. God grant that there may be no painful separations on that Great and Last Day. If we part then, we part to meet no more—parted for ever, or for ever united to the general assembly and church of the First Born which are written in heaven.

www.ingramcontent.com/pod-product-compliance
Lightning Source LLC
Chambersburg PA
CBHW021349230426
43666CB00006B/453